bread

bread

from sourdough to rye

Linda Collister

photography by **Martin Brigdale**

RYLAND
PETERS
& SMALL

LONDON NEW YORK

First published in the United States in 2001
by Ryland Peters & Small, Inc.
519 Broadway, 5th Floor
New York, NY 10012
www.rylandpeters.com

10 9 8 7 6 5 4 3 2

Printed and bound in China

ISBN 1 84172 208 1

Senior Designer Steve Painter
Commissioning Editor Elsa Petersen-Schepelern
Production Patricia Harrington
Picture Research Sarah Hepworth
Art Director Gabriella Le Grazie
Publishing Director Alison Starling

Food Stylist Linda Collister
Stylist Helen Trent
Indexer Hilary Bird

Author's acknowledgments
I would like to thank the following for their
help with this book:
Elsa Petersen-Schepelern, Steve Painter,
Martin Brigdale, Barbara Levy, Sarah
Lowman, Annette and Will Hertz, Michelle
Kershaw and Lakeland Limited for baking
equipment, Alan and Simon Silverwood of
Alan Silverwood Ltd for loaf tins and baking
trays. Pam Bewley for the Magimix food
processor, Helen Trent. And last but
certainly not least Alan Hertz.

Notes
All spoon and cup measurements are level unless
otherwise specified.

Before baking, weigh or measure all ingredients
exactly and prepare baking pans or trays.

Ovens should be preheated to the specified
temperature. Recipes in this book were tested
in 4 different kinds of ovens—all work slightly
differently. I recommend using an oven
thermometer and consulting the maker's handbook
for special instructions. To test a loaf, take it out
of the oven, tip it out of the pan, if any, and tap
it underneath. It should sound hollow like a drum.
If not return it to the oven for a little longer.

Library of Congress Cataloging-in-Publication Data

Collister, Linda.
  Bread : from sourdough to rye / Linda Collister ;
photography by Martin Brigdale.
     p. cm.
  Includes index.
  ISBN 1-84172-208-1
  1. Bread. I. Title.

TX769 .C562 2001
641.8'15 -- dc21   2001031776

contents

a simple pleasure ...

Can there be a simpler, purer pleasure than a loaf of good, freshly baked bread? Its aroma brings the house to life. Its flavor is memorable on its own, but enriches every food it accompanies. Its texture and crust thrill the mouth. Well-made bread is a treasure and making it brings many people peace and replenishment.

Bread is a staple in much of the world, but in many cultures bread is not taken for granted. It often plays an important role in religion and ritual. Because it is regarded as more than mere food, it is baked with the utmost care. Part of the fascination with bread —perhaps part of its religious significance—is the paradox of amazing variety emerging from utter simplicity. The basic ingredients—flour, salt, water, and usually leavening—are basic indeed, and they haven't changed since the Pharoahs. But by modifying the type of flour, or the liquid, or the leavening, by varying the temperature and rising times, you can create thousands of different breads. For example, the loaves of Northern Europe, heavy with rye and caraway and leavened with a sourdough starter, become altogether lighter when wheat flour is added. With a bit of experience and practice, you can use these recipes as starting points and create bread to suit your taste, your personality.

Another curiosity is bread's changing social significance. The ingredients are cheap enough, but the simple staples of peasants in one part of the world are dinner party sensations in another. When you dazzle your guests with focaccia or naan hot from the oven, you pay tribute to the value of traditional cultures, to their capacity to provide inexpensive but profound satisfactions. For those of us who live by the supermarket and the microwave, who call convenience culture civilization, baking bread can provide a lesson in humility.

The saying goes that all you need to make good bread is time, warmth, and love. It isn't true—you need good flour, too. Luckily the demand from craft bakers for high-quality flour has led to an increase in the range and availability of well-produced ingredients—flours, grains, and specialist cereals. Once you've tried baking with flour made from grain grown for flavor and milled with care, you will never use the bleached, highly refined, dirt-cheap stuff again. See page 142 for sources.

If you've never baked bread before, start with the Grant Loaf (page 82–85). There's little that can go wrong with this recipe; it needs no fancy ingredients or equipment or hours of work. It's incredibly nutritious and it tastes wonderful! Once you try bread you've baked yourself, you'll be hooked. I promise!

flour first ...

Bread requires flour, and exceptional bread requires high-quality flour. Any homemade bread will taste better than a supermarket loaf, but you need flour with real flavor to make good bread. Look for unbleached, organic flours from reputable millers.

To make flour, cereal grains have to be ground. There are two main ways to grind and mill the grains. A traditional stone mill, often powered by water or wind, crushes the grains between two large round stones. A roller mill, developed by the Swiss in the 1830s, rapidly grinds the grain between steel rollers, then separates the three elements of endosperm, bran, and germ. The bran is the dark outer husk of the kernel and contains minerals and fiber; it surrounds the endosperm which contains starch and protein, plus the germ or embryo, which is rich in oil and nutrients.

Wheat is the most common cereal used for home baking, but a wide range of flours from other cereals is available. Each has a distinct flavor and cooking characteristics, giving different taste and texture.

Wheat flour, the most important and popular flour for bread in the Western world, comes in many forms; for bread making you should buy flour labeled "all-purpose," "strong," or "for bread." This flour is made from hard wheat with a high proportion of protein to starch. The protein content determines how much gluten can be developed during kneading the dough. The gluten expands or stretches the dough as gases develop during fermentation, then sets in the heat of the oven to give a light-textured loaf. Check protein content on the side of the package —choose all-purpose flour with around 11.7 percent, or bread flour, 12–14 percent.

Whole-wheat flour Wheat flours are graded according to their extraction rate, usually stated on the side of the package, showing how much of the whole wheat kernel or grain is left in. Whole-wheat flour (100 percent extraction) is made from the complete wheat kernel, including the bran and germ. It is more nutritious with stronger flavor than white flour. Whole-wheat flours also vary in coarseness. Choose from stone-ground flour, finely milled, or coarsely milled flour (often used for Irish soda breads). The coarser the flour the more chewy and rough-textured the loaf will be. The high proportion of coarse golden flecks of bran in the flour means the loaf will be denser than one made with white flour, as the bran hinders the development of the gluten. White whole-wheat flour, popular in the US, gives a paler loaf and a milder flavor than regular whole-wheat flour.

Spelt flour is made from the spelt grain, found by archaeologists in many prehistoric sites and widely cultivated in Biblical times. It makes marvelous bread with a rich, nutty flavor and, although it comes from the same family as wheat, it has a different genetic structure, higher in protein and vitamins and minerals, and may be tolerable to people with wheat allergies. A popular organic flour.

Kamut is another ancient or heirloom wheat variety, available as whole-wheat and organic from Montana. It makes a golden loaf with a distinct taste, good in long-fermentation doughs.

Brown flour usually contains 85 percent of the whole-wheat kernel. **Farmhouse flour** has about 82 percent extraction, slightly less bran than brown flour, and gives a milder taste and lighter texture.

Cut wheat is the whole grain cut into 2–3 pieces, and can be added in small quantities to a dough to add extra texture.

Wheat flakes are made by steaming then rolling the kernel.

Graham flour is neither whole-wheat nor white, but halfway between. Large pieces of rolled whole wheat and bran give a beautiful flecked appearance and nutty flavor.

White flour usually has an extraction rate of 75 percent, with most of the bran and wheat germ removed. After milling, bleached flour is treated with chlorine dioxide to make it a bright white and to age the flour so it is rapidly ready for use. Unbleached flour is untreated, natural, and creamy, and is left to age to develop the baking qualities.

All-purpose flour is suitable for yeasted breads, soda breads, and recipes with chemical raising agents. For bread-making with yeasted breads, the protein content, listed on the side of the package, should be around 11.7 percent.

Self-rising flour contains chemical raising agents, normally baking powder. These react to moisture and the heat of the oven and produce bubbles of gas causing the flour mixture to rise.

High gluten bread flour is made from wheat with a high percentage of protein (usually 14 percent). It is used to make loaves that rise really well and is particularly good for bagels.

Italian-style or ciabatta flour is slightly gritty and makes a lively, supple dough, just what you need to produce the large air bubbles in ciabatta bread. The protein levels are usually about 10 percent.

French white flour, made from varieties particular to France, has slightly more protein, around 12 percent: Type 55 is the one used for making baguettes. French-style flours are also made in America.

Semolina flour is made from durum wheat, a very hard variety from the Mediterranean. The endosperm is finely ground to make a cream-colored flour that feels granular rather than powdery. It makes a tough, nutritious dough which is useful for pasta as it doesn't disintegrate in boiling water. It adds flavor and texture to bread doughs: replace up to 20 percent of the bread flour with semolina flour for Italian-style breads, pizza, and focaccia. Coarsely ground semolina meal (used to make semolina pudding) can be substituted for cornmeal in some recipes.

Cornmeal is made from the kernels of the corn or maize plant. Yellow and white cornmeals are made from the whole kernels ground to a fine, medium, or coarse texture—the coarser the texture the more crumbly the bread. Stone-ground cornmeal is highly prized by bakers for its texture and flavor. In the US, blue cornmeal, actually gray in color, is also popular and has a distinct taste. Very low in gluten, it must be mixed with wheat flours for yeasted breads but can be used alone for quick breads.

Cornstarch is a fine, white, powdery flour made by extracting the starch from the kernels. Gluten free and tasteless, it is used for sauces and mixed with wheat flour for baking. **Masa harina** is dried corn, treated with lime, then finely milled: used for tortillas. **Polenta**, by the way, is made from the corn kernel after the husk and the germ have been removed.

Rye flour was once a staple in Northern, Eastern, and Central Europe, where the soil was too poor or the conditions too cold to grow wheat. This gray-brown flour has very little gluten and makes a well-flavored but chewy, dark, and dense loaf that keeps well. For a lighter loaf, it is usually mixed with wheat flour. If you use a high proportion of rye flour, you also need a sourdough starter or an acidic element, like buttermilk or yogurt to break down the starch and let water be absorbed into the dough. For best texture and taste, choose stone-ground rye flour. **Light rye** is made by sifting out some of the bran; while **dark rye** is made from the whole grain, rather like whole-wheat flour. **Cut rye** is whole rye grain cut into 2 or 3 pieces and used for pumpernickel bread and to add flavor and texture to other doughs.

Flours shown left to right: spelt, white, organic rye, organic graham, organic whole-wheat.

a little bit of leaven ...

Leaven gives bread its texture and taste. It makes the dough rise and adds that instantly recognizable aroma and flavor of freshly baked bread.

Bread doughs can be raised in several ways, but most involve yeast. Yeast is a living organism, a single-celled fungus. To survive and multiply, the yeasts need the carbohydrates in the flour, the moisture added to flour to make the dough, and the air incorporated into the dough during kneading. The yeasts in turn produce alcohol and masses of tiny bubbles of carbon dioxide make the dough rise. Temperature is critical to their behavior—at very low temperature, the yeasts lie dormant; they thrive at around 78°F, grow very rapidly at 100°F, and are killed by anything over 140°F.

Sourdough starters have been used across the world for millennia to make well-flavored and well-risen bread. A naturally fermented starter is one made without commercial yeast. It can be a soft dough or a very thick runny batter, made from white bread flour, whole-wheat, or rye flour plus water. Wild yeasts are naturally present in the air and on grains, fruit, and vegetables, and a naturally fermented starter captures them and encourages them to grow. A healthy starter contains around 100 species of micro-organisms, a mixture of budding fungi or yeasts, and bacteria. The yeasts produce carbon dioxide gas needed to leaven the dough, plus a little alcohol which evaporates during baking; the bacteria produce lactic and acetic acids which slightly sour the dough, deepening the flavor. In rye flour doughs, these acidifiers break down the starch and give a much less sticky result.

Sourdough starters (page 13) come in many forms, but they all do the same thing—leaven and flavor the dough. They all need to be fed and watered regularly but can be used indefinitely if cared for. A white sourdough starter is multipurpose and can be used in any mixture, while a light rye flour starter is useful for rye loaves and for adding extra flavor to other doughs. Some French bakers use a rye starter plus white flour to make *pain ancien*—similar to *pain de campagne* (page 48). *Biga* is a saltless soft dough starter often used by Italian bakers to flavor their doughs. Most recipes include a small quantity of compressed yeast (usually ¼ oz. to 9 oz. flour and ½ cup water) to encourage fermentation. The mixture is left for 12 hours to mature—it must rise to 2–3 times its original volume and then collapse. A saved dough starter is literally that: after a dough has been proved and knocked back down, a piece is cut off and stored in an airtight plastic box in the refrigerator for up to a week. It is then brought back to room temperature and worked into the next batch of dough to leaven and flavor. The saved dough starter can be naturally fermented or yeasted, and made either from white flour or a mixture of flours. If you are using a recipe that calls for a saved dough starter, make up a batch of yeasted dough, cut off about 1 cup, put it in a plastic container, and refrigerate overnight to mature. The rest of the batch of dough can be used to make rolls or a small loaf.

Fresh compressed yeast is another common leaven. Given the choice I always use fresh yeast. I love its fragrance and texture and also think it makes better bread, with deeper flavor, aroma, and better keeping properties than dried yeast, though I can't prove this. It is available in some supermarkets, in the dairy aisle, or from craft bakers, and comes as a grayish-brown, putty-like block. The best way to store it is tightly wrapped in Saran-wrap in the dairy box in the refrigerator for up to 2 weeks or until the expiration date. If you buy a large block, say 2 lb., it's best to divide it into 0.6 oz. portions, wrap well, and freeze them. Defrost in the refrigerator for a couple of hours before use—but take care: if compressed yeast is left to defrost completely, it breaks down to a gluey liquid.

Most plain doughs use 1 oz. compressed yeast to 9 cups flour, though very sweet or rich doughs made with butter, fruit, or eggs need more. Adding extra yeast to a recipe can spoil the result rather than save time. Using less yeast than given means letting the dough rise longer, but this improves the flavor and may suit your timetable. To use compressed yeast, crumble it into a bowl or measuring cup and add some of the measured liquid. The liquid should be no more than warm and feel comfortable on the inside of your wrist. Too hot liquid will kill the yeast: too cool will just slow down its growth. The yeast liquid is then added to the flour with the remaining lukewarm liquid.

Active dry yeast is a light brown powder sold in ¼ oz. or 2-teaspoon packages, which equal 0.6 oz. compressed yeast. Store at room temperature or refrigerate. When opened, a package must be used at once. It is sprinkled onto the dry flour and mixed before liquid is added—it must not be stirred into the liquid. It works very quickly.

Dry yeast granules need to be proofed (mixed with water and sugar and left until frothy) before using. I have always found them more trouble than they are worth.

Temperature is crucial to a yeast dough—it likes moisture and gentle warmth. I put the mixed and kneaded dough back into the clean bowl, slip the bowl into a large plastic bag, inflate, and close tightly. I usually rise the dough on the kitchen counter at around 70°F. To slow down the process, the dough can be left to rise overnight in the refrigerator or a cold room. If you are in a hurry, leave it above a warm stove, in a sunny spot, or in a warming cupboard at no more than 95°F and check frequently. The dough should only double in size—if it grows more, it may collapse in the oven. Doughs that prove slowly usually have better taste and texture and keep longer than quickly made doughs. However, heavy, enriched doughs do need warmth to encourage the yeast to grow.

Non-yeast leavens—a simple, quick way to make a bread dough is to add chemical raising agents—baking powder, baking soda, or cream of tartar. When mixed with suitable liquid (baking soda needs something acidic: cream of tartar something alkaline) and warmth, they produce gases. The dough doesn't have to be kneaded or left to rise, so these are often called quick breads. Instead the bread is baked immediately before the chemical reaction is complete.

using electric mixers

Free-standing mixers—many bread doughs can be mixed and kneaded using a heavy-duty free-standing food mixer. Always follow the maker's instructions, fit the dough hook, and use the quantity of flour which is recommended by the manufacturer (usually no more than about 4½ cups). Use the lowest speed and work the dough for no more than about 5 minutes. Most doughs can be made in a free-standing mixer—though not quick breads, muffins, or tortillas. As a rule, any recipe that tells you to knead the dough can be put in the mixer.

Food processors—though some people do make bread in a food processor, I have never had any success in the processors I have tried.

making a sourdough starter

The aim is to capture and grow natural yeasts—fungi—present in the air and on the flour. As they grow, they produce bubbles of carbon dioxide gas and lactic acid, which will eventually be used to leaven the dough and add flavor. For best results use unbleached organic flour—I use white flour for a multi-purpose starter, but rye or whole-wheat flours can also be used. I recommend that you use spring water. If you use tap water, you should filter, boil, and cool it first. The kitchen counter is usually the best place to raise a starter.

to begin

¼ cup all-purpose flour

½ cup tepid water (see recipe introduction above)

for each refreshment

¼ cup all-purpose flour

tepid water (see recipe introduction above)

Put the flour and water in a small bowl and mix to a thick sticky paste. Cover the bowl with a damp cloth such as cheesecloth and secure with an elastic band—don't cover the bowl with plastic wrap. Leave it in a draft-free spot on a kitchen counter, re-dampening the cloth as necessary.

After 2–4 days (depending on conditions) the paste should have a skin and look bubbly. It should have a milky scent. If it smells bad rather than slightly sour, or if you can see patches of mold, or if there are no signs of life, throw it away and start again.

At this stage, you should give your starter its first feed or refreshment. Add another ¼ cup flour and enough tepid water to make a soft, sticky paste-like dough. Work the dough with your hand or a wooden spoon to get plenty of air into the mixture. Cover the bowl again with a damp cloth and leave it, as before, for 24 hours.

The starter should look very active now. Stir well then remove and discard half of it. Add another ¼ cup flour and enough tepid water to make a dough as before. Cover and leave as before for 12 hours.

At this point, the sourdough starter should look very active and ready to use—to ensure there is enough to make a batch of bread and keep some for the next batch, you will need to increase the volume. You can do this by eye or by measuring—you will need about ¼ cup flour and enough water to make a soft sticky dough as before. After 4–6 hours, the dough

should be bubbly again and ready to use. However, if the dough doesn't look active enough to use after its previous refreshment, you will need to halve it once more and feed it as before.

Once you have got a starter going, it will keep forever. If you look after it, you may never have to buy yeast or bread again. Feed it regularly, every 5 days or so, even if you are not using it (you can give away rather than discard half each time). Store it in a plastic container or glass jar in the refrigerator. When you want to use it, bring the starter back to room temperature, then feed it about 6 hours before starting the recipe. It should turn bubbly again.

To make a very vigorous but mild-tasting sourdough starter, halve and feed it, once it is established, every 6–8 hours until it is very bubbly. If your starter has become very sour smelling, a bit stale, or slow working, or if you haven't baked for a couple of weeks, then you can get it back to health in the same way.

Note: Don't worry if your starter separates into a darkish liquid layer on top of a thicker paste. Just stir it up and feed as normal. This happens if you haven't fed the starter for a while, or if the starter is runny.

If it smells strongly and makes your eyes water, then it is in bad shape. Reduce it to a couple of tablespoons, then add flour and water in the same proportions as before every day until the starter is bubbly and has a milky aroma.

basic bread making

The best way to start baking bread is to make this basic loaf several times to get a feel for the dough. But watch out! The kick you get from taking beautiful bread out of the oven is addictive. There's not much that can go wrong—you can kill the yeast with too much heat, but over-handling is not a problem as it is with pastry. Bread dough is very accommodating; you can fit rising times into your plans by varying the rising temperatures.

basic loaf step-by-step

4⅔ cups all-purpose flour

1½ teaspoons sea salt

1¾ cups tepid water

0.6 oz. cake compressed yeast*

a large baking sheet, greased

makes 1 large loaf

* To use active dry yeast, mix one ¼ oz. package with the flour and salt, then continue as in the main recipe.

1 Mix the flour and salt in a large bowl. In cold weather, warm the flour in a low oven, 300°F for a few minutes—this will give the yeast a flying start.

Alternatively, you can warm the flour in a microwave on HIGH for 15 seconds.

2 Put the water in a measuring cup or bowl and crumble the yeast over the top. The water should be no warmer than blood heat or the yeast will be killed off, so test it with your hand. I prefer to use boiled and cooled filtered tap water because it has less chlorine and chemicals, but other bakers use spring water.

3 Pour the yeast liquid and the rest of the tepid water into the well in the flour.

4 Work the mixture with your hands until it comes together to make a ball of dough that leaves the sides of the bowl and your hands clean. It should feel firm.

If the dough feels soft and sticky, work in a little extra flour, 1 tablespoon at a time: if it feels dry and crumbly and there are crumbs in the bottom of the mixing bowl, then work in a little more liquid, 1 tablespoon at a time. Some recipes will require a soft dough—this gives a more open-textured loaf.

5 Turn out the dough onto a lightly floured work surface and knead thoroughly for 10 minutes. The dough must be stretched to develop the gluten in the protein in the flour into long strands. These will expand, along with the gas bubbles the yeast produces, to give a light and risen dough, not a heavy, flat scone.

To knead the dough, first use the heel of your hand to stretch it away from you, as if pulling out a rubber band; then gather it back into a ball. Turn it around and repeat the process until it feels very elastic.

6 To test if the dough is sufficiently kneaded, stretch a little of the dough between the thumb and forefinger. It should be very elastic and silky smooth and stretch to paper-like, almost translucent thinness.

7 Return the dough to the bowl, then cover tightly with plastic wrap or a lid and let rise until doubled in size. Allow 1 hour in a warm spot, 1½ hours at normal room temperature, 2–3 hours in a cool place, or overnight in the refrigerator.

8 Don't let the dough over-prove or it may collapse in the oven later on. When the dough has risen properly, it won't spring back if you press it with your finger.

9 Punch down the risen dough a couple of times to deflate, or turn it out the onto a lightly floured work surface before punching.

The large bubbles of air will be redistributed so the final loaf is even-textured. Some recipes skip this stage as the loaf is intended to have holes in it—ciabatta for example.

• Replace half the white flour with an equal quantity of stone-ground whole-wheat bread flour for a well-flavored loaf with a good texture, not too heavy.

• For a 100 percent whole-wheat loaf, use 4⅔ cups stone-ground whole-wheat bread flour. The dough will be heavier to work and the bread closer in texture and heavier, but it will have a rich flavor.

• For a softer crumb, mix the dough with tepid milk instead of water.

• Replace some or all of the white flour with spelt or kamut for a deeply flavored, nutty loaf with extra goodness.

• Replace a quarter of the all-purpose flour with rye flour. All rye flour will make a much heavier loaf.

10 Gently knead and shape the dough into a neat ball, but try not to work it too much at this stage: a rough shape is better than a tough loaf.

11 Set the loaf on the prepared tray—it can also be shaped into a cylinder and set in a large, greased loaf pan, 16 x 5 x 4 inches. Slip the tray or pan into a large plastic bag and let rise in a warm spot until doubled in size.

At this stage, the yeast likes to be in a warm and humid environment and a plastic bag slightly inflated and closed with a peg or wire tie is ideal. Allow 45 minutes–1 hour, or longer if the dough has been in the refrigerator.

Meanwhile, preheat the oven to 425°F.

12 Uncover the loaf and slash the top several times with a sharp knife or a razor blade.

Bake in the preheated oven for 35 minutes until the loaf is golden brown.

13 To test if the loaf is thoroughly cooked, turn it upside down using a thick cloth or oven gloves, then tap with your knuckles on the underside. It should sound hollow, like a drum. If it sounds heavy and dead, then return it to the oven, bake for 5 minutes more, then test again.

Transfer the bread to a wire rack and let cool completely before slicing.

the americas

The Americas owe their diverse cuisines to two factors: an unprecedented mix of peoples and cultures, and, in North America, the huge range of foods available—produced in some of the best growing conditions in the world.

The most famous American bread has to be cornbread, which has been developed from native American origins. Quickly made with stone-ground corn, flavored with bacon fat or hot peppers, plus fresh corn kernels and eaten hot from the skillet, it is loved by cowhands and bond traders alike, proving that fast food can be both delicious and wholesome.

Rye, along with corn, was another cereal cultivated by the early settlers on the East Coast. Some loaves made with the heavy dough, such as Boston Brown Bread, were steamed in a pot over the fire. Later, Jewish immigrants from southern Germany to the New York area brought their own, very different, recipes. They also introduced America to the bagel and it is now found throughout all fifty states. With the cultivation of the great wheatfields of the Midwest prairie states, wheat flour took over as king, leading the way for light, airy doughnuts and California Sourdough, with good-quality flour and real, live starter, rather than a sachet of flavoring.

Supermarkets and natural food stores stock an immense variety of flours and grains, yeasts and seeds. I urge those wedded to commercial bakeries and breadmaking machines to try making one of these American classics in the traditional way.

If you have eaten only the ordinary supermarket versions, these rich white rolls with their soft crumb and crust, ideal for splitting and filling, will astonish you. They do justice to the finest burger or chili dog. I use them for Maine lobster rolls, my summer lunch treat.

hamburger buns and hot dog rolls

4⅓ cups all-purpose flour

1 tablespoon salt, preferably sea salt

2 teaspoons sugar

3 tablespoons unsalted butter, diced

0.6 oz. cake compressed yeast*

1⅔ cups tepid milk

1 large egg, beaten

sesame seeds, to sprinkle

to glaze

3 tablespoons milk

a good pinch of salt

several baking sheets, greased

makes 18

* To use active dry yeast, mix one ¼ oz. package with the flour, salt, and sugar. Add the milk and egg and continue as in the main recipe.

Mix the flour, salt, and sugar in a large bowl. Add the butter and rub in with the tips of your fingers until the mixture looks like fine crumbs. Make a well in the center.

Crumble the yeast into a small bowl, then stir in about a quarter of the milk to make a smooth liquid. Pour into the well with the rest of the milk and the egg. Gradually work the flour into the liquid to make a soft but not sticky dough. If the dough feels sticky, work in a little more flour, 1 tablespoon at a time: if there are dry crumbs in the bowl, or the dough feels tough and dry, work in a little more tepid milk, 1 tablespoon at a time.

Turn out the dough onto a lightly floured work surface and knead thoroughly for 10 minutes until silky smooth and very pliable. Return the dough to the bowl, cover with plastic wrap, and let rise in a warm but not hot place, until doubled in size, about 1 hour.

Turn out the risen dough onto a lightly floured work surface and punch down to deflate. Divide the dough into 18 equal pieces.

To make hamburger buns, shape the dough into balls, then cup your hand over one ball, so your fingertips and wrist touch the work surface. Gently rotate your hand so the dough underneath is rolled around and smoothed into a neat, even ball. Gently flatten to make a bun about 4 inches across.

To make hot dog rolls, shape each piece into a cylinder or sausage about 6 inches long, then gently taper the ends by squeezing with the edges of your hands.

Set the pieces of shaped dough slightly apart on the prepared trays, then slip the trays into a large plastic bag, inflate, seal, and let rise as before until almost doubled in size, about 45 minutes. Meanwhile, preheat the oven to 450°F.

Uncover the dough and lightly brush with the milk mixed with the salt. Hamburger buns can also be sprinkled with sesame seeds.

Bake in the preheated oven for 5 minutes then lower the temperature to 400°F and bake for a further 5–10 minutes until golden brown and firm. To keep the crusts soft, cool on a wire rack covered with a dry cloth.

Best eaten within 24 hours, or toasted. Can be frozen for up to 1 month.

california sourdough

There seem to be more recipes for California and San Francisco sourdough than there are bakers in the state. Before a loaf was shaped and baked, the original pioneers and settlers kept back a portion of dough to leaven the next batch. These days bakers use a range of leavens; saved dough starter, soupy sourdough leavens, fresh yeast, dried sourdough flavorings, or baking soda. The objective is a light-textured, mildly sour, well-risen white loaf. The authentic flavor comes from the foggy atmosphere and the water of the area, which are hard to reproduce, but this is a good approximation.

1 cup sourdough starter (page 12)*

2 cups tepid water

0.6 oz. cake compressed yeast**

6 cups all-purpose flour

2 teaspoons salt, preferably sea salt

2 baking sheets, greased

makes 2 medium loaves

* If you don't keep a sourdough starter, use a small piece of dough, about ¾ cup or 6 oz., saved from a previous batch of bread. Gradually work in enough tepid water to make a very soft dough, cover, and leave for 8 hours at room temperature, then use 1 cup for the starter for this recipe.

** To use active dry yeast, mix one ¼ oz. package with the flour and salt, then work it into the sourdough starter and water mixture.

Put the starter and water into a large bowl and mix with your hand to make a soupy batter. Crumble the yeast and work it into the mixture. Mix the flour with the salt, then gradually beat into the liquid with your hand until well mixed. The dough should feel soft but not sticky: if it feels too slack, work in extra flour, 1 tablespoon at a time: if it feels hard or dry, or there are crumbs left in the bottom of the bowl, work in extra water, 1 tablespoon at a time.

Turn out onto a floured work surface and knead thoroughly to make a smooth, firm, very supple dough. Return the dough to the bowl and cover with plastic wrap. For the best flavor, let rise slowly in a cool room until doubled in size, about 4 hours, or overnight in the refrigerator.

Turn out onto a lightly floured work surface and punch down to deflate (if dough has been stored in the refrigerator, let it come back to room temperature before continuing, 1½–2 hours).

Divide the dough into 2 equal pieces, cover with plastic wrap, and let rest for 10 minutes. Shape each piece into a neat ball, handling the dough as little as possible. Put onto the prepared trays, then slide into a large plastic bag, slightly inflate, and close the end. Let rise at normal room temperature until almost doubled in size, about 2 hours.

Meanwhile, preheat the oven to 425°F. Put a roasting pan of water into the oven to heat: the steam created will help develop a good crust.

Uncover the loaves and quickly slash the top in a diamond pattern using a small serrated knife or a razor blade. Put into the heated, steamy oven and bake for 30 minutes or until the loaves sound hollow when tapped underneath. Cool on a wire rack.

Eat within 5 days or toast. Can be frozen for up to 1 month.

This is the light-textured but well-flavored bread my husband remembers from his childhood, and by which he judges every loaf. It makes excellent sandwiches, is good with smoked salmon (sorry, lox!) and is excellent toasted. Early Dutch bakers in New Amsterdam used caraway seeds along with rye flour—the wheat flour we now take for granted was once too expensive for everyday use. The yogurt develops the rye and helps fermentation.

new york rye

Mix the flours, salt, and caraway seeds in a large bowl. Make a well in the center. In cold weather take the chill off the flour by gently warming it in a low oven for a few minutes, or in the microwave for a few seconds.

Crumble the yeast in to a small bowl, add about a quarter of the water, and stir until dispersed. Pour into the well in the flours along with the rest of the water and the yogurt. Gradually draw the flours into the well to make a soft but not sticky dough: flours vary, so if it feels too slack, work in extra white flour, 1 tablespoon at a time, or if it feels hard or dry, or there are crumbs left in the bottom of the bowl, work in extra water, 1 tablespoon at a time.

Turn out the dough onto a lightly floured work surface and knead thoroughly for 10 minutes until it feels very pliable. Return the dough to the bowl, cover with plastic wrap, and let rise in a warm place until doubled in size, about 2 hours.

Turn out the risen dough onto a lightly floured work surface and punch down to deflate. Divide the dough into 2 equal pieces and shape each into an oval. With the edge of your hand, make a good crease down the center of each dough oval, then roll it over to make an oval sausage. Turn the dough over on the work surface so the seam is underneath and the top looks smooth and evenly shaped. Put the shaped loaves on the prepared tray. Slip them into a large plastic bag and inflate slightly. Let rise as before until doubled in size, about 1½ hours.

Meanwhile, preheat the oven to 425°F. Uncover the loaves and slash the tops with a sharp knife. Bake in the preheated oven for 35 minutes, or until they sound hollow when tapped underneath. Cool on a wire rack.

Best eaten within 5 days. Can be frozen for up to 1 month.

2½ cups rye flour

4⅔ cups all-purpose flour

2 teaspoons salt, preferably sea salt

2 teaspoons caraway seeds

0.6 oz. cake compressed yeast*

2¾ cups tepid water

2 tablespoons plain yogurt, at room temperature

2 baking sheets, greased

makes 2 medium loaves

* To use active dry yeast, mix one ¼ oz. package with the flours, salt, and caraway seeds, then add the water and yogurt and continue as in the main recipe.

new york bagels

Bagels, the New York bread that won over America, originated in southern Germany. They then migrated to the Polish shtetl where they became a popular, everyday bread sold by street hawkers. But the Jewish delicatessens of New York made the roll with the hole—the bangle—a household name. The famous spongy texture and chewy glossy crust is the result of briefly boiling the risen dough rings just before baking. Choose your favorite topping—or a mixture of them all. If possible, use special (very high protein) bread flour.

3¼ cups all-purpose flour or bread flour

2 teaspoons salt, preferably sea salt

one 0.6 oz. cake of compressed yeast*

2 teaspoons malt syrup

1⅛ cups tepid water

1 large egg, beaten

2 tablespoons melted butter or vegetable oil

to finish

1 tablespoon malt syrup, for poaching

1 egg white, lightly beaten, for glazing

sesame seeds, poppy seeds, sunflower seeds, caraway seeds, or onion flakes, for sprinkling

several baking sheets, greased

makes 12

* To use active dry yeast, mix one ¼ oz. package with the flour and salt. Make a well in the center, add the liquid ingredients, and continue with the recipe.

step-by-step

1 Put the flour and salt in a large bowl, mix well, then make a well in the center.

2 Crumble the yeast into a small bowl, add the malt syrup and half the water, and stir until completely dispersed.

3 Pour into the well in the flour, together with the rest of the water, the egg, and the melted butter or oil.

4 Using your hand, mix these ingredients in the well, then gradually draw in the flour to make a soft and pliable dough. If tough and dry, work in more water. Leave the dough to rest for 5 minutes.

5 Turn out the dough onto a lightly floured work surface and knead thoroughly for 10 minutes until very smooth and elastic. Return the dough to the bowl, then put the bowl inside a large, slightly inflated plastic bag, or cover the bowl with plastic wrap and let rise at normal room temperature until doubled in size, about 1½ hours.

6 Punch down the risen dough with your knuckles, then it out onto a floured work surface and divide into 12 equal portions. Shape into neat balls, then cover with a dry cloth and let rest for 5 minutes.

7 Flatten the balls slightly with your fingertips.

8 Flour a forefinger and push it through each ball to make a ring shape. Twirl and rotate the dough to make the hole larger—it will close up during cooking.

9 Arrange the bagels well apart on a floured baking sheet covered with a dry cloth. Set aside for 15 minutes.

Meanwhile preheat the oven to 400°F.

10 Bring a large saucepan of water to a boil. Add the malt syrup and stir well. Gently drop in the bagels 2–3 at a time and poach in the boiling water for 30 seconds.

Turn them over with a slotted spoon and, after a further 30 seconds, lift them out. Drain thoroughly, then set onto greased baking sheets.

11 When all the bagels have been poached, brush with the lightly beaten egg white, taking care not to glue the dough to the tray.

12 Leave plain or sprinkle with your chosen topping. Bake in the preheated oven for 20–25 minutes until golden. Remove from the oven and let cool on a wire rack.

Best eaten within 1 day. Can also be split and toasted.

The traditional New England Friday night supper used to be Boston baked beans, frankfurters, and a dark, slightly sweet and sticky, steamed bread made with equal quantities of rye, whole-wheat flour, and cornmeal. Though the bread was traditionally steamed over the beans and sausages, on a recent visit I found the best bakeries in the area now bake it in the oven, which improves both flavor and texture. However the bread and beans combination remains as popular as ever.

boston brown bread

1 cup stone-ground whole-wheat flour

1¼ cups stone-ground dark rye flour

1⅛ cups stone-ground cornmeal

½ teaspoon salt, preferably sea salt

¾ teaspoon baking powder

1½ teaspoons baking soda

½ cup unsulphured dark molasses

2 cups milk

1 clean coffee can about 4½ inches diameter and 7 inches deep, well greased and lined with parchment paper, or small deep cake pan (see recipe)

makes 1 medium loaf

Preheat the oven to 300°F.

Put the flours, cornmeal, salt, baking powder, and baking soda into a large bowl and mix thoroughly. Make a well in the center.

Gently warm the molasses with the milk, stir until dissolved, then pour into the well in the dry ingredients. Using a wooden spoon, gradually work the dry ingredients into the liquid to make a thick, smooth batter.

Spoon the mixture into the can.* The container should be about three-quarters full.

Bake in the preheated oven for 1¼–1½ hours or until a skewer inserted in the center comes out clean. Cool for 5 minutes, then gently ease the bread out of the pan. Cool on a wire rack.

Eat while still warm from the oven, or the same day.

Variation: For a sweeter loaf add ½ cup raisins or dried cranberries to the batter, mix well, then spoon into the can and bake as given.

*Note: You can also use a deep, 7-inch cake pan extended in height by 4 inches with a collar of heavy-duty aluminum foil, well buttered on the inside, then secured with a paper clip. Alternatively, use an ovenproof glass 8-cup French coffee press insert.

You know it's Spring in Vermont when the maple syrup mills go to work. This loaf combines two favorite American ingredients to make a bread rich in flavor, but not too sweet. Using whole-wheat flour and roasting the pecans enhances the nuttiness. A good breakfast bread, or with ham or cheese for sandwiches.

maple pecan loaf

2½ cups stone-ground whole-wheat flour

2⅓ cups all-purpose flour

2 teaspoons salt, preferably sea salt

2 cups pecans, lightly toasted and coarsely chopped

0.6 oz. cake compressed yeast*

1½ cups tepid water

½ cup maple syrup

2 standard loaf pans, 9 x 5 x 3 inches, lightly greased

makes 2 medium loaves

* To use active dry yeast, mix one ¼ oz. package with the flours, salt, and nuts; then add the water and syrup to the bowl and continue as in the main recipe.

Mix the flours, salt, and nuts in a large mixing bowl and make a well in the center. Crumble the yeast into a small bowl, pour in half the water, then stir until thoroughly dispersed. Pour into the well, followed by the rest of the water and the maple syrup. Mix the ingredients in the well, then gradually work in the flour to make a soft but not sticky dough. If the dough sticks to your fingers, work in extra flour, 1 tablespoon at a time: if the dough feels stiff and dry or there are crumbs in the base of the bowl, work in a little more water, 1 tablespoon at a time.

Turn out the dough onto a lightly floured work surface and knead thoroughly for 10 minutes until very elastic. Return the dough to the bowl, cover with plastic wrap, and let rise in a warm place until doubled in size, about 1½ hours.

Turn out the risen dough onto a lightly floured work surface and punch down to deflate. Divide the dough into 2 equal pieces and shape each into a loaf to fit the pans. Set a loaf into each prepared pan, then slip the pans into a large plastic bag, slightly inflated. Close, then let rise as before until doubled in size, about 45 minutes–1 hour.

Meanwhile, preheat the oven to 400°F.

Bake the uncovered loaves in the preheated oven until they are a good golden brown and sound hollow when turned out and tapped underneath, about 30–35 minutes. Turn out and let cool on a wire rack.

Best eaten within 4 days or toasted. Can be frozen for up to 1 month.

poppy seed challah

The elaborately plaited Sabbath loaf, sometimes made with up to twelve strands of dough, was first made by the Jews of Central Europe in the Middle Ages. The soft, sweet dough, enriched with eggs, honey, and fat, made a complete contrast to the coarse, hard, and slightly bitter daily bread. The Jews took challah on their migrations first to Eastern Europe, then to the West. Here the dough is fashioned into a four-strand plait and finished with poppy seeds.

4⅔ cups all-purpose flour

2 teaspoons sea salt

0.6 oz. cake compressed yeast*

⅞ cup tepid water

3 medium eggs, beaten

3 tablespoons honey

⅓ cup sunflower oil or unsalted butter, melted and cooled

to finish

1 egg, beaten with a pinch of salt

2 teaspoons poppy seeds

a large baking sheet, greased

makes 1 large loaf

* To use active dry yeast, add one ¼ oz. package to the flour with the salt, then proceed with the recipe.

step-by-step

1 Put the flour and salt in a large bowl, mix well, then make a well in the center.

2 Put the water in a measuring cup or small bowl, then crumble the yeast over the top and stir until dispersed.

3 Pour into the well in the flour, then add the eggs, honey, and oil or butter. Mix the ingredients in the well, then gradually work in the flour to make a soft but not sticky dough. If too dry, work in tepid water 1 tablespoon at a time: if too sticky, work in extra flour, 1 tablespoon at a time.

4 Turn out the dough onto a floured work surface and knead thoroughly for 10 minutes until very smooth and elastic.

5 Return the dough to the washed and lightly oiled bowl, then turn the dough over so the surface is coated in a thin film of oil—this will prevent a skin forming. Slip the bowl into a slightly inflated plastic bag and seal, or cover with plastic wrap. Let rise until doubled in size, about 1½ hours at normal room temperature, or overnight in the refrigerator.

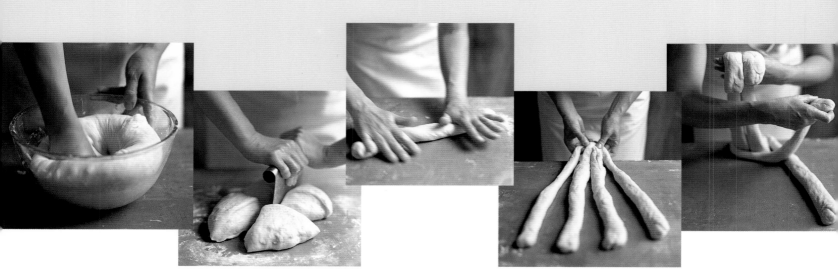

6 Punch down the risen dough to deflate, then cover and let rise again until doubled in size, about 45 minutes at normal room temperature (allow longer if the dough has been chilled).

7 Turn out the dough onto a floured work surface, and punch down to deflate. Divide into 4 equal pieces.

8 Using your hands, roll each to a rope about 16 x 1 inch thick.

9 Pinch the ropes firmly together at one end, then arrange vertically in front of you, side by side, slightly apart with the join on top.

10 Run the far-left strand under the 2 middle ones.

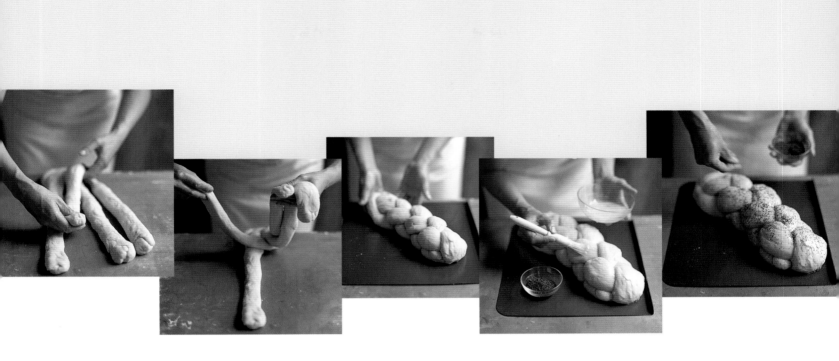

11 Run it back over the last it went under.

12 Run the far-right strand under the twisted 2 in the middle, then back over the last one it went under.

Repeat until all the dough is plaited. Pinch the ends together at the bottom.

13 Transfer to the prepared baking sheet, then slip the tray into a large plastic bag, slightly inflated. Let rise at normal room temperature until almost doubled in size, about 45 minutes. Meanwhile, preheat the oven to 425°F.

14 Carefully brush the loaf with 2 thin coats of the egg glaze.

15 Sprinkle with the poppy seeds. Bake for 10 minutes in the preheated oven, then reduce the temperature to 375°F and bake for a further 30 minutes or until the loaf is golden brown and sounds hollow when tapped underneath. Cool on a wire rack.

Best eaten within 4 days. The cooled loaf can be frozen for up to 1 month.

breakfast doughnuts

Old recipe books contain many recipes for doughnuts: they made a quick and substantial fresh breakfast. Today, coffee and doughnuts have a place of affection in the early-morning American consciousness. These are based on old Irish settler recipe and—rather than a yeast dough—use mashed floury potatoes for speed and flavor. The spices make this recipe my absolute favorite—I make it to celebrate Hannukah.

Mix the flour with the salt, spices, baking soda, and sugar in a large bowl. Rub in the butter with the tips of your fingers until the mixture looks like crumbs.

Add the mashed potatoes, work in briefly, then work in the eggs and enough of the buttermilk to make a soft, biscuit-like dough. If the dough feels very sticky, work in extra flour 1 tablespoon at a time.

Turn out the dough onto a lightly floured work surface and knead for a few seconds until it is just smooth. Roll it out ½-inch thick, then cut out rounds using the larger cutter. Stamp out the center of each round with the smaller cutter. Re-roll the trimmings and center circles, then cut out more rings.

Fill a large saucepan with frying basket one-third full with the oil (or a deep-fryer to the manufacturer's recommended level). Heat the oil 350°F, or until a small cube of bread will brown in 40 seconds. Fry the doughnuts 2 or 3 at a time, turning them frequently, until well browned and cooked through, about 4 minutes. Remove from the oil with a slotted spoon and drain well on paper towels.

Mix the cinnamon sugar ingredients together, sprinkle over the doughnuts, then serve warm with coffee.

Best eaten within 24 hours.

3 cups all-purpose flour

¼ teaspoon salt, preferably sea salt

½ teaspoon ground ginger

½ teaspoon ground cinnamon

½ teaspoon freshly grated nutmeg

1½ teaspoons baking soda

1 cup sugar

3 tablespoons unsalted butter, diced

1 cup firmly packed mashed potatoes (very smooth)

2 large eggs, beaten

1 cup buttermilk (or a mixture of half plain yogurt and half lowfat milk)

vegetable oil, for frying

cinnamon sugar

2 tablespoons sugar

1 teaspoon ground cinnamon

3-inch round plain cookie cutter

1-inch round plain cookie cutter

makes 12

A delicious, yeasted cornbread recipe made with fresh corn, mild jalapeño chiles, and tangy mature cheese—choose Monterey Jack or Cheddar. Serve with Mexican omelets, with salads, or for sandwiches.

fresh corn jalapeño and cheese bread

3¼ cups all-purpose flour

½ cup whole-wheat bread flour

1⅛ cups coarse cornmeal

1 cup corn kernels, fresh or frozen and thawed

1½ teaspoons salt, preferably sea salt

1⅓ cups grated cheese

2 scallions, finely sliced

2 jalapeño chiles, seeded and finely chopped

0.6 oz. cake compressed yeast*

1⅓ cups tepid water

1 large egg, beaten

1 tablespoon honey

*2 standard loaf pans,
9 x 5 x 3 inches, greased*

makes 2 medium loaves

* To use active dry yeast, mix one ¼ oz. package with the dry ingredients then add the water, honey, and egg and finish as in the main recipe.

Put the flours, cornmeal, corn, salt, cheese, sliced scallions, and chopped chiles in a large bowl and mix well. Make a well in the center.

Crumble the yeast into the tepid water, stir until thoroughly dispersed, then pour into the well. Mix the egg and honey into the liquid. Gradually work the dry ingredients into the yeast liquid to make a heavy, soft, but not sticky dough. If the dough feels sticky, work in a little more flour, 1 tablespoon at a time: if there are dry crumbs in the bowl, or the dough feels tough and dry, work in a little more tepid water, 1 tablespoon at a time.

Turn out onto a lightly floured work surface and knead thoroughly for 5 minutes.

Return the dough to the bowl, cover with plastic wrap, and leave in a warm place until doubled in size, about 1½ hours.

Turn the risen dough onto a lightly floured work surface and punch down to deflate. Divide the dough into 2 equal pieces and shape each into a cylinder to fit your pans. Set the dough neatly in the pans, then slip them into a large plastic bag, inflate slightly, and seal. Let rise as before until doubled in size, about 1 hour.

Meanwhile, preheat the oven to 400°F. Uncover the loaves and bake in the preheated oven for 30 minutes until golden and the turned out loaves sound hollow when tapped underneath. Cool on a wire rack.

Best eaten within 4 days. Can be frozen for up to 1 month.

Freshly made cornbread is an American classic, to be eaten with chili, stews, and soups. This recipe is quick to assemble and flavored with corn kernels, cracked black pepper, and hot red pepper flakes.

two pepper cornbread

1¼ cups coarse yellow cornmeal

1 cup all-purpose flour

½ teaspoon salt, preferably sea salt

½ teaspoon black peppercorns

½ teaspoon hot red pepper flakes

2 pinches of ground cumin

2 teaspoons baking powder

1 large egg

1 cup milk

1¼ cups corn kernels, fresh or frozen and thawed

8-inch square cake pan, well greased

**makes 1 medium loaf:
6–8 portions**

Preheat the oven to 400°F.

Put the cornmeal, flour, and salt into a mixing bowl. Crack the peppercorns with a mortar and pestle or spice grinder (a coffee grinder kept for the purpose)—make them as coarse or fine as you like. Add to the bowl with the pepper flakes, cumin, and baking powder and mix thoroughly. Make a well in the center.

Beat the egg and milk in a bowl or measuring cup, then pour into the mixing bowl. Stir gently to make a coarse-looking batter—do not beat or overmix or the cornbread will be tough. Briefly stir in the corn, then spoon into the prepared pan.

Bake in the preheated oven for about 20 minutes until firm and golden. Turn out onto a bread board, cut into large squares, and eat warm from the oven. If not eating immediately, cool on a wire rack, but eat within 24 hours.

Fresh Green Chile and Cumin Cornbread
For a milder variation, omit the black peppercorns and hot red pepper flakes. Add 1 small mild green chile, seeded and finely chopped, and 1 teaspoon lightly toasted cumin seeds.

tortillas

The name is the Spanish conquistadors' distortion of *tlaxcalli*, the Nahuatl word for a thin, circular, unleavened bread. Corn tortillas are traditionally made from fresh corn that has been soaked in slaked lime to loosen the husks, then ground very finely to make a fine fresh meal called masa. This is then shaped and pressed into a thin disk and cooked on hot stones or a flat metal plate. Without fresh masa, corn tortillas are made from masa harina, lightly roasted dried masa dough, and more difficult to work. Wheat flour tortillas are popular in the north of Mexico, other parts of Latin America, and the Southwest. They are fairly easy to make, and even easier to become addicted to.

flour tortillas

1⅔ cups all-purpose flour

¼ cup fine whole-wheat flour

½ teaspoon salt, preferably sea salt

2 pinches of ground cumin

freshly ground black pepper

1 teaspoon baking powder

3 tablespoons lard or vegetable shortening, diced

about ⅔ cup warm water

corn tortillas

2 cups masa harina

¼ teaspoon salt, preferably sea salt

1⅓ cups tepid water

1 tablespoon freshly squeezed lime juice

a flat-surfaced griddle or large skillet, ungreased

makes 8

To make flour tortillas, mix the flours, salt, spices, and baking powder in a bowl. Rub the diced fat into the flour with the tips of your fingers, until the mixture looks like fine crumbs. Gradually work in enough of the water to make a soft but not sticky dough. Cover the bowl with plastic wrap and let rest for 30 minutes.

Divide the dough into 8 equal pieces and shape into neat balls. Roll out on a well-floured work surface to make very thin disks about 8 inches across. Alternatively, use a tortilla press.

To make corn tortillas, mix the cornmeal with the salt in a bowl. Mix in the water and lime juice to make a clammy soft dough. If the dough is a bit crumbly, work in a little more water, 1 tablespoon at a time: if it's too sticky, add more cornmeal—getting the right consistency takes practice. Cover the dough in plastic wrap and leave for 30 minutes before attempting to roll out.

Divide the dough into 8 equal pieces, then shape into balls. Pat each one flat and slap from palm to palm until about it becomes a thin disk about 6½ inches across. The balls of dough can also be flattened in a tortilla press. (As a student I had to make over a hundred for a party, without a press, and I found the easiest way to flatten the dough was to set each ball between two pieces of plastic wrap on the work surface, then press down and flatten the dough with a small, heavy pan.)

Heat an ungreased griddle or heavy skillet over medium heat, then cook the tortillas, one at a time, for about 1 minute on each side for wheat tortillas, or 1–2 minutes on each side for corn tortillas, or until brown blisters appear.

Keep the tortillas warm under a folded cloth while cooking the rest of the batch.

Eat warm as soon as possible.

france, italy, and spain

Wheat has been cultivated around the Mediterranean for longer than in any other part of Europe. The conditions needed for wheat—well-drained soil and plenty of hot sun—are nearly perfect. So a host of wheat varieties thrive in the great diversity of soils and microclimates, leading to some interesting and highly individual breads.

Italy's durum wheat was famous even in Roman times. The semolina flour made from durum not only makes the best pasta, but, when mixed with a softer wheat flour, gives Italian bread its particular taste and texture.

Wheat varieties grown by French farmers produce entirely different results, from the lively baguette dough which makes a razor-sharp, crisp crust and light but chewy crumb to the hearty *pain de campagne* with its thick rustic crust and moist, heavier crumb. White flour is king here—whole-wheat bread still brings back memories of wartime deprivations.

For most people in the Mediterranean, a meal without bread would be unthinkable. Breakfast means a sweet roll or toasted day-old baguette with coffee. Lunch is a slice of pizza or stuffed focaccia and salad. Snacks like tapas are based on bread, and entrées at dinner are incomplete without it.

pain de campagne

The large, crusty, chewy, well-flavored loaf found in the best bakeries in France is made from a flour that retains a small proportion of bran to give an off-white color. It's almost impossible to buy this flour outside of specialist wholesale millers, so I've added some whole-wheat pastry flour to the white flour. Choose an organic flour for the best results and use filtered tap water that's been boiled and cooled (or spring water) to avoid a chlorine taint. Feed the starter about 6 hours before starting the recipe to make sure it's vigorous.

3 cups all-purpose flour

¼ cup fine whole-wheat pastry flour

1½ teaspoons salt, preferably sea salt

1 cup soft dough sourdough starter (page 13)

about 1⅓ cups tepid water

a baking sheet or pizza baking stone

makes 1 large loaf

Mix the flours and salt in a large bowl, then make a well in the center. Spoon the starter into the well, then pour in the water. Mix the starter with the water to make a soupy batter, then gradually work in the flour to make a slightly soft dough. Depending on the consistency of the starter, you may need to work in a little extra flour or water, 1 tablespoon at a time.

Turn out onto a lightly floured work surface and knead thoroughly for 10 minutes until very smooth and elastic.

Return the dough to the bowl, cover with plastic wrap, and let rise in a warm place until doubled in size, about 2–6 hours depending on the vigor of your starter and the temperature. The dough can also be left to rise in a cool room or the refrigerator overnight.

Turn out the risen dough and punch down to deflate. Shape the dough into a rough ball and dust with flour. Set the dough in a linen-lined proving basket or a basket or colander lined with a well-floured linen cloth. Slide the basket into a large plastic bag and inflate slightly. Let rise in a warm place until doubled in size, about 2–4 hours. The dough will take longer if it has been in the refrigerator.

Towards the end of the rising time, preheat the oven to 450°F. Put a heavy baking sheet or pizza stone into the oven to heat.

Uncover the loaf and turn out onto the hot tray or stone, then quickly slash the top with a small sharp knife or blade. Put into the preheated oven—if you have a water spray or mister bottle, quickly spray the oven to create a burst of steam. Bake until the loaf turns a dark golden brown and sounds hollow when tapped underneath, about 30–35 minutes. Cool on a wire rack.

Best eaten within 5 days or toasted. Can be frozen for up to 1 month.

baguettes

Good French bread depends on the right flour, a good hot oven, and a bit of steam. French bakers use type 55 flour —like US French-style flour (*see* mail order, page 142).

Put half the flour and half the salt into a large bowl or plastic bowl with a lid. Put the water in a measuring cup or bowl, crumble in a quarter of the yeast, and stir until dispersed. Add the yeast liquid to the flour and work it with your hand to make a very smooth, thick batter. Cover tightly with the lid or plastic and leave at normal room temperature until doubled in size and very bubbly, about 8 hours or overnight.

Next day, uncover the bowl and stir the mixture well. Put 1 tablespoon of tepid water into a measuring cup or bowl and crumble the remaining yeast over the top: stir to disperse. Add to the batter, then work in the rest of the flour and the salt to make a firm dough. If the dough feels sticky, work in a little more flour, 1 tablespoon at a time, if there are dry crumbs in the bowl, or the dough feels tough and dry, work in a little more tepid water, 1 tablespoon at a time.

Turn out the dough onto a work surface and knead very thoroughly for 10 minutes until the dough feels very elastic. Put the dough back into the bowl, cover, and leave as before until doubled in size, about 1 hour.

Carefully turn out the dough onto a work surface. Without punching it down or handling the dough too much, divide it into 3 equal pieces and shape each one into a rough ball. Cover with a dry cloth and let rest for 15 minutes.

Using a lightly floured rolling pin, roll out each ball to about 9 x 12 inches, then roll up tightly like a jelly roll. Tuck in the ends and pinch the seam together securely. Put on an unfloured work surface, then roll up with your hands like a sausage, until it just fits on your baking sheet and looks neat and smooth with gently tapered ends.

Lightly flour a large, dry cloth and put it on a large tray or board. Carefully set each loaf on the cloth, pleating the cloth in between each loaf to make a barrier and support. Cover the tray with a large sheet of plastic and let rise as before until doubled in size, about 40 minutes. Meanwhile preheat the oven to its hottest setting and put a roasting pan of water and the baking sheet in to heat.

Gently and carefully roll the risen loaves onto the heated trays. Make 4 slashes along the loaves with a small sharp knife. Set the trays in the oven and spray with water using a mister. Shut the oven as quickly as possible. Bake for 20 minutes until very golden and crisp, spraying with water again after the first 5 minutes. Tip the loaves off the trays onto the oven racks and bake for 2–3 minutes more for a really crisp crust. Cool on a wire rack.

Eat the same day. Not suitable for freezing.

3 cups French white flour, type 55, or French-style flour (*see* page 142 for suppliers)*

1 teaspoon salt, preferably sea salt

0.6 oz. cake compressed yeast**

1¼ cups tepid water, either filtered or spring water

a roasting pan

a large baking sheet

makes 3 medium loaves

* If you are unable to buy American French-style flour, all-purpose flour may be used, but the baguettes will not be as authentic in texture.

** To use active dry yeast, use one ¼ oz. package. Mix one-quarter of the package with half the flour and half the salt, then add all the water as given for the first stage. Mix the remaining yeast with the rest of the flour and salt, add to the batter, and continue as in the main recipe.

olive and thyme bread

Eat this bread warm, with the best extra virgin olive oil and balsamic vinegar you can afford for dipping, and some wine for sipping. A very relaxed way to start a meal.

This is also good bread for serving with antipasti or for mopping up delicious salad dressings.

I developed this recipe after seeing beautiful similar loaves in bakeries in the South of France. Basically I wanted a bread stuffed with plump, oily black olives (choose the plumpest, richest olives you can find). The whole point of this loaf is the high proportion of crust to crumb, just made for snacking—perfect with a glass of wine on a fine summer evening in the garden before dinner.

1½ cups all-purpose flour

3 tablespoons fine whole-wheat flour

1 teaspoon sea salt

⅔ cup sourdough starter (page 13)

about ⅔ cup tepid water

scant 1 cup good quality black olives, such as kalamata or niçoise, pitted

2 teaspoons fresh thyme leaves, stripped from the stalks

a baking sheet, greased

makes 1 medium loaf

1 Put the flours and salt in a bowl and mix.

2 Make a well in the center and add the starter and water.

3 Work the starter and water together to make a soupy mixture, then gradually work in the flour to make a slightly soft dough. Depending on the consistency of the starter, you may need to work in a little extra white flour or water.

4 Turn out onto a lightly floured work surface and knead for 10 minutes until very pliable and smooth.

5 Return the dough to the bowl, cover with plastic wrap, and let rise in a warm spot until doubled in size, about 3 hours depending on the vigor of the starter.

6 Punch down the risen dough a couple of times to deflate, or turn it out onto a lightly floured work surface before punching down.

7 Using your knuckles, gently pat the dough into a narrow rectangle about 16 inches long.

8 Sprinkle the olives and thyme down the middle of the dough.

9 Fold over the sides to enclose the filling.

10 Pinch the seam to seal in the filling, then gently roll the dough with your hands to make a sausage about 2 feet long.

11 Carefully lift the dough onto the prepared sheet and shape into a ring, joining the ends. Slip the sheet into a large plastic bag, slightly inflate, then let rise in a warm spot until doubled in size, about 2 hours.

Meanwhile, preheat the oven to its maximum setting, and put a roasting pan of water in the bottom to create a steamy atmosphere.

12 Uncover the ring and slash lightly with a sharp knife or razor blade. Put into the hot oven and, if possible, spray with water to increase the steam.

Bake until the loaf is a good brown, very crisp, and sounds hollow when tapped underneath, 8–15 minutes depending on your oven. Cool on a wire rack.

Eat warm within 24 hours. The cooled loaf can be frozen for up to 1 month.

An old recipe from Provence, where filleted anchovies, preserved in salt then canned or bottled, are a favorite ingredient in all sorts of savory dishes—vegetable, meat, or fish. Serve this bread with fish soups or salads.

anchovy and olive oil bread

Put ⅔ cup of the tepid water into a large bowl and crumble the yeast over the top. Work in 1⅛ cups of the flour to make a thick, smooth batter. Cover with plastic wrap and leave for 30 minutes until puffy and sponge-like.

Meanwhile, put the anchovies and olive oil in a small saucepan and heat gently, stirring over the lowest possible heat, until melted and paste-like, about 5 minutes. Stir in the brandy and let cool.

Uncover the sponged dough and work in the rest of the tepid water, the remaining flour and salt, then finally the cooled anchovy mixture to make a very soft dough.

Turn out onto a floured work surface and knead for 5 minutes.

Return the dough to the bowl, cover with plastic wrap, and let rise in a warm place until doubled in size, about I hour.

Turn out the risen dough onto a floured work surface and punch down to deflate. Shape into a disk 8 inches in diameter. Set on the prepared tray, slip the tray into a large plastic bag, inflate, seal, and let rise as before until doubled in size, about 40 minutes.

Meanwhile, preheat the oven to 425°F.

To finish, uncover the risen dough, gently press your fingers into the dough to dimple the surface, then press the anchovies into the dimples. Sprinkle the oil over the dough, then bake in the preheated oven for about 25 minutes until the loaf is golden and sounds hollow when tapped underneath. Transfer to a wire rack to cool.

Best eaten the same day or the next, or toasted. Can be frozen for up to 1 month.

0.6 oz. cake compressed yeast*

1 cup tepid water

3¼ cups all-purpose flour

¼ cup extra virgin olive oil

15 anchovy fillets, rinsed and finely chopped

1 tablespoon brandy

½ teaspoon salt, preferably sea salt

to finish

2 tablespoons olive oil

6 anchovy fillets, rinsed and coarsely chopped

a large baking sheet, greased

makes 1 large loaf

* To use active dry yeast, mix one ¼ oz. package with the first 1⅛ cups flour, then stir in the ⅔ cup water. Continue as in the main recipe.

Ciabatta comes from Northern Italy, around Lake Como, and has become almost as popular and ubiquitous as the baguette. The roughly shaped bread has a floury crust, a moist open texture, and a good flavor of fruity olive oil. It can be difficult to make at home—for the best results use an Italian-style ciabatta flour, which is granular and quite coarse in texture. This helps create a lively dough producing the large air bubbles needed for the characteristic texture. The biga, an Italian aged-dough starter, adds extra flavor.

ciabatta rolls

To make the biga, put the flour into a large bowl and make a well in the center. Crumble the yeast into the well, then pour in the water. Mix the yeast with the water, then gradually work in the flour to make a firm dough. Turn out onto a work surface and knead for 2 minutes, then return the dough to the bowl and cover with plastic wrap. Leave at normal room temperature for 8–12 hours—the dough will rise up enormously, then fall back.

The next day, to make the ciabatta dough, put the 1⅓ cups tepid water in a measuring cup or bowl and crumble the whole cake of compressed yeast over the top. Stir well until dispersed. Add to the biga and work into the dough by stirring and squeezing with your fingers to make a thick, smooth batter.

Work in half the flour to make a very sticky, batter-like dough, then beat with your hand for 5 minutes until the dough has been thoroughly stretched and become very elastic. Cover the bowl and let rise in a warm place until about 2½ times its original size, about 2 hours.

Add the salt and oil to the dough, then gradually work in the rest of the flour to make a rather soft, sticky dough. When the dough feels smooth and very elastic, cover the bowl and let rise in a warm place as before, this time until doubled in size, about 1 hour.

Meanwhile preheat the oven to 450°F. Gently warm the baking sheets.

Gently tip the risen dough onto a well-floured work surface. Using a well-floured bread scraper, divide the dough into 12 pieces and transfer to the trays, spaced well apart. If necessary, shape into rough-looking rolls with well-floured fingers. Dust heavily with flour, then slip the trays into large plastic bags, slightly inflated.

Let rise in a warm place for about 30 minutes until almost doubled in size—don't worry if the dough also spreads out.

Uncover the rolls, then bake for 15–20 minutes until golden brown and crisp. Cool on a wire rack.

Eat warm from the oven or within 1 day. Can be frozen for up to 1 month.

biga

1¾ cups all-purpose flour

one-third of a 0.6 oz cake compressed yeast*

⅔ cup tepid water

ciabatta dough

1⅓ cups tepid water

0.6 oz. cake compressed yeast*

3¼ cups all-purpose or Italian-style flour flour

2 teaspoons salt, preferably sea salt

¼ cup virgin olive oil

several baking sheets, heavily floured

makes 12 rolls

* To use active dry yeast, mix one-third of a ¼ oz. package with the flour to make the biga, then work in the water. Finish the biga as in the main recipe. To make the ciabatta dough, add the water to the biga and work in to make a batter. Then mix half the four with one ¼ oz. package active dry yeast, add to the batter, and finish as in the main recipe.

Homemade pizza is a real treat and great fun. Since everyone can add their own touches, this is a good way to introduce children to cooking.

pizza and pizzette

3¼ cups all-purpose flour

1 teaspoon salt, preferably sea salt

1 teaspoon herbes de Provence

freshly ground black pepper

0.6 oz. cake compressed yeast*

1¼ cups tepid water

1 tablespoon extra virgin olive oil

2-inch round plain cookie cutter

several baking sheets or a pizza stone

makes 6 thin pizzas, 4 thick pizzas or about 30 pizzette

* To use active dry yeast, mix one ¼ oz. package with the flour, salt, and herbs, then add the water and oil and continue as in the main recipe.

Mix the flour with the salt, dried herbes de Provence, and a few grinds of black pepper in a mixing bowl, then make a well in the center.

Put the tepid water in a measuring cup or bowl, crumble the yeast over the top, and stir thoroughly until dispersed. Stir in the oil, then pour the mixture into the well in the flour. Gradually work the flour into the yeast liquid to make a soft dough.

Turn out onto a floured work surface and knead thoroughly for 10 minutes until very supple and elastic. Return the dough to the bowl, cover with plastic wrap, and let rise until doubled in size, about 1 hour in a warm place or overnight in the refrigerator.

Turn out the risen dough onto a floured work surface and punch down to deflate. If making individual thin pizzas, divide the dough into 6 equal pieces. Using well-floured hands, pat and pull out each piece of dough to a thin circle slightly smaller than a dinner plate. For thick crust pizzas divide the dough into 4, then pat out each piece to a disk ½ inch thick. Put the dough circles on a surface liberally sprinkled with cornmeal or flour, cover them with plastic wrap or a dry cloth, and leave to prove for 15 minutes. If making the mini pizzas, roll out the dough to about ¼ inch thick, and cut out rounds with the cookie cutter.

Turn the oven to its highest setting and put in the baking sheets or a pizza stone to heat while you prepare the toppings, about 30 minutes, depending on your oven. Add the toppings of your choice, then quickly transfer the pizzas to the hot trays or pizza stone. Bake for 8–10 minutes until crisp and browned. (Small pizzette will take slightly less time.) Remove with a long-handled spatula and eat the pizzas immediately.

Tomato, Mozzarella, and Oregano Topping
Tip 14 oz. canned chopped tomatoes into a strainer set over a bowl and let drain (save the juice for a soup or sauce). Transfer to a food processor, add 2 tablespoons tomato purée, 2 tablespoons extra virgin olive oil, 3 crushed garlic cloves, and 1 tablespoon chopped fresh oregano leaves. Blend to a purée. Add salt, pepper, lemon juice, or hot red pepper flakes to taste. Spoon over the pizzas, then top with about 6 oz. sliced mozzarella cheese.

Gorgonzola, Thyme, and Onion Topping
Heat 3 tablespoons extra virgin olive oil in a medium, heavy skillet, then stir in 4 large, finely sliced onions, 1 tablespoon fresh thyme leaves, and 1 bay leaf. Cut a disk of waxed paper to fit inside the skillet, then press it down on top of the onions. Cover with a lid and cook over very low heat for 35 minutes. Uncover the softened onions, stir well, and cook over medium heat, stirring very frequently, until they are a light golden brown and no longer watery. Add a splash of white wine to balance the richness and season with a little salt and plenty of pepper. Boil until the wine has almost evaporated, then remove from the heat. Discard the bay leaf and let cool. Spread over the prepared and slightly risen pizza rounds, then scatter 12 oz. cubed Gorgonzola cheese over the top.

stuffed focaccia

This variation on a famous Italian classic makes piquant picnic food—simple to prepare, transport, and eat. Alternatively, serve it warm for lunch in the garden with a glass of red or a chilled white wine.

0.6 oz. cake compressed yeast*

1⅛ cups tepid water

6 tablespoons extra virgin olive oil

about 3¼ cups all-purpose flour

2 teaspoons chopped fresh sage leaves

2 teaspoons salt, preferably sea salt

freshly ground black pepper

spinach, chile, and anchovy filling

3.75 oz. jar anchovy fillets in olive oil, drained and rinsed

1 cup young spinach leaves

1 or 2 medium-hot red chiles, such as serrano, seeded and finely sliced

freshly ground black pepper

a rectangular pan, about 12 x 7½ inches, oiled

makes 1 large bread

* To use active dry yeast, mix one ¼ oz. package with all the flour and flavorings, then work in the oil and the water. If the dough feels dry, work in more water, 1 tablespoon at a time; if too sticky, add more flour, 1 tablespoon at a time. Proceed as in the main recipe.

To make the focaccia dough, crumble the yeast into a mixing bowl. Pour in the water, stir until dispersed, then add 3 tablespoons of the oil. Add half the flour, then the sage, salt, and pepper. Mix to make a sticky wet dough. Gradually work in enough of the remaining flour to make a very soft but not sticky dough.

Turn out onto a floured work surface and knead thoroughly for 10 minutes until very elastic and slightly firmer.

Return the dough to the bowl, cover with plastic wrap, put in a warm place, and let rise until doubled in size, about 1 hour.

Turn out the risen dough onto a floured work surface and punch down to deflate. Divide the dough in half. Press and pat out one piece to fit the base of the prepared pan. Arrange the anchovies evenly over the dough. Season with a little black pepper, then cover with the spinach leaves. Sprinkle as much sliced chile over the top as you like.

Roll or pat out the second piece of dough to a rectangle to fit the pan, then set it on top of the filling. Press down gently to expel as much air as possible, then pinch together the top and bottom edges of the dough to seal in the filling completely. Prick the top layer with a skewer or toothpick to release any bubbles of air trapped inside. Cover and let rise as before until doubled in size, about 45 minutes.

Meanwhile, preheat the oven to 425°F.

Brush the remaining olive oil over the risen focaccia, then bake in the preheated oven for 20–25 minutes until crisp and golden brown. Remove from the pan immediately and cool on a wire rack.

Eat warm or at room temperature the same day. Not suitable for freezing.

A rich, sweet, light-textured Italian breakfast bread flavored with oranges. It is made with pine nuts and hazelnuts in Southern Italy and with almonds in Sardinia. The nuts are gently toasted for maximum flavor.

pignola

scant 1 cup golden raisins

the grated zest and juice of 2 organic oranges

2¾ cups all-purpose flour

1 teaspoon salt, preferably sea salt

1¼ sticks unsalted butter, diced

2 large eggs, beaten

2 tablespoons tepid water

0.6 oz. cake compressed yeast*

¼ cup hazelnuts, lightly toasted in a dry skillet

¾ cup pine nuts, lightly toasted in a dry skillet

confectioners' sugar, for dusting

a baking sheet, well greased

makes 1 large loaf

* To use active dry yeast, mix one ¼ oz. package with the flour after the butter has been rubbed in. Add the eggs and golden raisin mixture plus 2 tablespoons water; then continue as in the main recipe.

Put the golden raisins, orange zest, and juice in a bowl and let soak overnight.

Next day, mix the flour and salt in a large bowl. Rub the diced butter into the flour with the tips of your fingers until the mixture looks like coarse crumbs. Make a well in the center, then add the beaten eggs and the soaked golden raisin mixture.

Put the tepid water in a bowl, crumble the yeast over the top, and mix to a smooth liquid. Pour into the well in the flour. Mix the yeast, eggs, and golden raisins together in the well, then gradually work in the flour to make a very soft, slightly sticky dough. If there are dry crumbs in the bowl, or the dough seems dry and tough, work in a little more tepid water, 1 tablespoon at a time.

Turn out the dough onto a floured work surface. Knead for 5 minutes. It will be soft and pliable but not as sticky. Return it to the bowl, cover with plastic wrap, and let rise in a warm place until doubled in size, about 3 hours, or overnight in the refrigerator.

Turn out the risen dough onto a floured work surface, sprinkle with the nuts, and gently work them in. When they are evenly distributed, shape the dough into a ball, then pat into a round about 8 inches diameter and 1½ inches thick. Set onto the prepared baking sheet. Slip the tray into a large plastic bag, inflate slightly, then let rise in a warm place until doubled in size, about 1 hour. Allow longer if the dough has been in the refrigerator.

Meanwhile, preheat the oven to 375°F.

Uncover the dough and bake in the preheated oven for about 35 minutes until the loaf is golden brown and sounds hollow when tapped underneath. Transfer to a wire rack, dust with confectioners' sugar, and let cool.

Eat within 4 days or freeze for up to 1 month.

pan de nueces

In late Fall, the sight of fresh walnuts in the markets of Southern Europe heralds the baking of breads, cakes, and tarts. To get the best out of the nuts—fresh or from a package—roast them in the oven until lightly browned and wonderfully aromatic. This simple, sweet, unyeasted loaf comes from Spain, but I've eaten similar ones in France, Italy, and Greece, served with a cup of coffee.

2 cups shelled walnuts

2 tablespoons unsalted butter, softened

1 tablespoon walnut oil

scant 1 cup sugar

1 large egg, lightly beaten

2 cups all-purpose flour

a good pinch of salt

1 teaspoon baking powder

1⅛ cups milk

1 loaf pan, 9 x 5 x 3 inches, greased and lined with baking parchment

makes 1 medium loaf

Preheat the oven to 350°F.

Put the walnuts into a roasting pan or baking dish and toast in the preheated oven until lightly browned, about 15–20 minutes. Let cool, then coarsely chop in a food processor or with a large, sharp knife.

Cream the butter, oil, and sugar in a mixing bowl, then work in the egg. Beat the mixture thoroughly for 1 minute, then add the nuts. Sift the flour, salt, and baking powder into the bowl, then add the milk. Stir well to make a sloppy batter.

Pour into the prepared pan and bake in the preheated oven for about 40 minutes or until golden brown and a skewer inserted in the center comes out clean.

Turn out on to a wire rack and let cool. Wrap and keep for 1 day before slicing.

Best eaten within 5 days. Can be frozen for up to 1 month.

northern and eastern europe

Across the top of Europe, where the climate was too cold, wet and inhospitable for wheat, the farmers grew rye. The obstinate flour was transformed with the aid of sourdough starters into dark, dense loaves with a deep flavor. Today rye breads come in all hues and the despised grain of the rural poor is fashionable among the urban rich. The perfect match for smoked or cured fish and meats, for pungent cheeses, or rustic soups, rye breads made traditionally with sourdough, or in the modern way with some yeast and wheat flour, are eaten far away from their original home—or rather hovel.

In northern Europe, fine-textured, creamy, white wheat flour was once used on a daily basis only by the rich; for everyone else, sweet white bread was a treat. Spicy hot cross buns, sticky rich Chelsea buns, the wonderfully aromatic *vetebrod* and *saffronsbrod* of Scandinavia, and the Polish poppy seed loaf are all heirloom recipes, once made only for holidays. Now, the staple food and the holiday treats of the poor, as well as the delicacies of the wealthy, are available to all of us all the time. Make and enjoy them!

Bread flavored with leeks or onions plus cheese and sage is commonly found in Wales and the West of England. My local cheese store tells me that *caws Caerffili* (Caerphilly cheese), cut in cake-like wedges, was traditionally eaten underground by Welsh coal miners. It is a moist, crumbly, milk-white cheese with a salty tang—Asiago is a good substitute in this recipe. Eat this bread with soup and salads or use to make great ham sandwiches.

welsh cheese and leek bread

1 large leek, trimmed, cleaned and finely chopped, about 5 oz. prepared weight

2 tablespoons unsalted butter

a good pinch of dried sage or 1 teaspoon chopped fresh sage (optional)

freshly ground black pepper

1⅔ cups all-purpose flour

1⅔ cups stone-ground whole-wheat flour

1½ teaspoons salt, preferably sea salt

1⅓ cups tepid milk and 1 cup tepid water, mixed

0.6 oz. cake compressed yeast*

1 cup Asiago cheese, crumbled

to glaze

3 tablespoons milk

a good pinch of salt

cracked wheat berries or oatmeal, for sprinkling

2 baking sheets, greased

makes 2 round loaves

* To use active dry yeast, mix one ¼ oz. package with the flours and salt, then add the milk and water mixture and continue as in the main recipe.

Carefully rinse and drain the chopped leeks. Melt the butter in a medium skillet. Add the leek, sage, and pepper and cook slowly, stirring occasionally, until softened, about 15 minutes. Cool until barely warm.

Mix the flours and salt in a large bowl and make a well in the center. Put the tepid milk and water mixture into a bowl or measuring cup, crumble the yeast over the top, and stir until completely dispersed. Pour into the well, then gradually work in the flour to make a soft dough. If the dough feels sticky, work in a little more flour, 1 tablespoon at a time: if there are dry crumbs in the bowl, or the dough feels tough and dry, work in a little more tepid milk or water, 1 tablespoon at a time.

Turn out the dough onto a lightly floured work surface and knead thoroughly for 10 minutes until very pliable. Gently work in the leek mixture until thoroughly and evenly mixed, then flatten the dough until it is about 1 inch thick. Crumble the cheese onto the dough. Cut the dough into 3 equal pieces and stack them together, pressing down well. Cut the stack in half, then put one piece on top of the other and press down. Return the dough to the bowl, cover with plastic wrap, then let rise in a warm place until doubled in size, about 1 hour.

Turn out the dough onto a lightly floured work surface and punch down to deflate. Divide into 2 equal pieces and gently shape each into a disk, about 6 inches diameter. Set on the prepared trays. Slip the trays into a large plastic bag and inflate slightly. Let rise as before until almost doubled in size, about 45 minutes.

Meanwhile, preheat the oven to 425°F.

Uncover the loaves and brush lightly with the milk mixed with the salt. Sprinkle with the cracked wheat berries or oatmeal. Bake the loaves in the preheated oven for 25 minutes or they are until golden brown and sound hollow when tapped underneath. Cool on a wire rack. Eat while still warm or reheat gently.

Best within 4 days, or toasted. Can be frozen for up to 1 month.

old-fashioned cottage loaf

My great-grandmother made this recipe a hundred years ago. It has a moist chewy crumb and a good crunchy crust and baking it will fill the house with a most wonderful smell. This is a real treat!

4⅔ cups all-purpose flour

2 teaspoons salt, preferably sea salt

2 tablespoons unsalted butter, diced

0.6 oz. cake compressed yeast*

1 rounded teaspoon honey

1¾ cups tepid water

1 egg, beaten, to glaze

a large baking sheet, greased

makes 1 large loaf

* To use active dry yeast, mix one ¼ oz. package with the flour and butter mixture, then add the honey and tepid water, and mix as in the main recipe.

Mix the flour and salt in a large bowl. Add the butter and rub in with the tips of your fingers until the mixture looks like fine crumbs. Make a well in the center.

Crumble the yeast into a small bowl, add the honey and about a quarter of the water, then stir until smooth and creamy. Pour the mixture into the well, then add the rest of the tepid water. Gradually work the flour into the liquid in the center to make a slightly firm dough—if it is soft it won't keep its shape later on. If the dough feels sticky or soft, work in extra flour, 1 tablespoon at a time.

Turn out the dough onto a lightly floured work surface and knead thoroughly for 10 minutes until the dough feels very pliable, smooth, and elastic.

Return the dough to the bowl, then cover with plastic wrap or slip the bowl into a large, slightly inflated plastic bag. Seal, then let rise at normal room temperature (not a warm or hot place) until doubled in size, about 1½–2 hours.

Turn out the risen dough onto a lightly floured work surface and punch down with your knuckles. Cut off one third of the dough, then gently knead and shape both pieces of dough into balls. Put, well apart, on a well-floured work surface, covered with plastic wrap or a very slightly damp cloth, then let rise until almost doubled in size, about 45 minutes–1 hour.

Meanwhile, preheat the oven to 450°F.

Gently lift the larger ball onto the baking sheet and flatten it slightly. Gently flatten the smaller ball and set it on top. Push 2 fingers and a thumb joined together down into the middle of the loaf to press both pieces together. Leave for about 5–10 minutes longer, then brush lightly with the beaten egg to glaze—avoid glueing the loaf to the tray. Using a small sharp knife or razor blade, score all around the edge of both balls.

Bake in the preheated oven for 15 minutes, then lower the temperature to 400°F and bake for about 20 minutes longer until the loaf sounds hollow when tapped underneath. Cool on a wire rack.

Best eaten within 5 days or toasted. Can be frozen for up to 1 month.

These flat oval rolls with their soft, fine crumb and floury soft top (crust is somehow the wrong word) are much loved by people of Scottish descent. They can be filled with crisp broiled bacon for breakfast, or with salad to make a filling snack. The recipe may also be flavored with cooked bacon or herbs and garlic.

floury baps

4⅔ cups all-purpose flour

2 teaspoons salt, preferably sea salt

4 tablespoons unsalted butter, diced

0.6 oz. cake compressed yeast*

good ¾ cup tepid milk

1⅛ cups tepid water

extra milk, for brushing

extra flour, for dusting

2 baking sheets, greased

makes 12

* To use active dry yeast, mix one ¼ oz. package with the flour and salt, then add the butter and continue as in the main recipe.

Mix the flour and salt in a large bowl. Rub the diced butter into the flour using the tips of your fingers until the mixture looks like fine crumbs, then make a well in the center.

Crumble the yeast into a small bowl, pour in the tepid milk, and stir until dispersed. Pour into the well in the flour, then pour in the tepid water.

Gradually draw the flour into the well and mix to make a slightly soft dough. If the dough feels sticky, work in a little more flour, 1 tablespoon at a time: if there are dry crumbs in the bowl, or the dough feels tough and dry, work in a little more tepid water, 1 tablespoon at a time.

Turn out the dough onto a lightly floured work surface; knead thoroughly for 10 minutes until very smooth and elastic. Return the dough to the bowl and cover with plastic wrap. Let rise until doubled in size, about 1 hour in a warm kitchen, 1½ hours at normal room temperature or overnight in the refrigerator.

Turn out the risen dough onto a lightly floured work surface, and punch down to deflate. Divide into 12 equal pieces and gently roll or pat each to an oval or circle slightly less than ½-inch thick and about the size of a saucer. Set well apart on the prepared trays, then lightly brush with milk. Dredge with flour, then slip the trays into large plastic bags, inflate slightly, then seal. Let rise until just doubled in size, about 30 minutes in a warm kitchen.

Meanwhile preheat the oven to 425°F.

Uncover the baps and press down in the center of each with your thumb. Dust the tops again with flour, then bake in the preheated oven for about 12–15 minutes until golden. Let cool on a wire rack covered with a dry cloth.

Eat while still warm or within 24 hours, or toasted. Can be frozen for up to 1 month.

Herb garlic baps Add ¼ cup chopped fresh herbs (any combination of parsley, cilantro, tarragon, rosemary, chervil, thyme, oregano, chives, lovage, or basil) and 2 garlic cloves, thinly sliced, after rubbing in the butter and before adding the liquids.

Fried bacon baps Sauté or broil 4 slices bacon until crisp. Drain, then crumble or chop finely. Add to the rubbed-in mixture with a few grinds of pepper and the grated zest of ½ orange.

extra-spicy hot cross buns

Traditionally marked with a cross made from pastry or cut into the dough, these rich spicy fruit buns are eaten on Good Friday. However, ancient Egyptians offered similar small yeast cakes to the goddess of the moon, while the Greeks and Romans made them for the goddess of light, a custom taken up by the Saxons who added the cross. Cook them for breakfast on Good Friday and serve them warm, then have them toasted the next day with tea or coffee.

step-by-step

3 cups all-purpose flour

⅛ cup stone-ground whole-wheat bread flour

¼ cup sugar

1 teaspoon sea salt

1 teaspoon apple pie spice

½ teaspoon freshly grated nutmeg

4 tablespoons unsalted butter, diced

⅔ cup dried currants

⅓ cup golden raisins

¼ cup chopped mixed peel

0.6 oz. cake compressed yeast*

1¼ cups tepid milk

1 extra-large egg, beaten

pastry cross

⅛ cup all-purpose flour

1½ tablespoons unsalted butter, diced

2 teaspoons sugar

to glaze

¼ cup milk

3 tablespoons sugar

2 baking sheets, greased

makes 12

* To use active dry yeast, mix one ¼ oz. package with the flours and salt; then rub in the butter, add the dried fruits and peel, add the liquids, and proceed with the recipe.

1 Put the flours, sugar, salt, and spices in a large bowl and mix well.

2 Add the diced butter and rub into the flour using the tips of your fingers until the mixture looks like fine crumbs.

3 Mix in the dried fruit and mixed peel, then make a well in the center of the mixture.

4 Crumble the yeast into a small bowl, pour in about half of the milk, and stir until completely dispersed.

5 Add to the well in the flour with the rest of the milk and the egg. Gradually draw in the flour to make a soft but not sticky dough. If the dough sticks to your fingers or the bowl, work in a little extra flour, 1 tablespoon at a time; if the dough feels stiff and dry, work in a little milk or water, 1 tablespoon at a time.

6 Turn out the dough onto a lightly floured work surface and knead thoroughly for 10 minutes.

7 Return the dough to the bowl, then put the bowl into a large plastic bag and inflate slightly, or cover the bowl with plastic wrap. Let rise in a warm spot in the kitchen until doubled in size, about 1½ hours.

8 Punch down the risen dough a couple of times to deflate, or turn it out onto a lightly floured work surface before punching down.

9 Divide the dough into 12 equal pieces. Shape each into a neat ball and set well apart on the greased trays. Slip the sheets into large plastic bags and inflate slightly or cover with a slightly damp cloth and let rise as before until doubled in size, about 45 minutes–1 hour.

Meanwhile, preheat the oven to 400°F.

10 To make the pastry for the cross, put the flour, butter, and sugar into a small bowl and rub the butter into the flour with the tips of your fingers until the mixture looks like coarse crumbs. Stir in 1–2 tablespoons cold water to make a firm dough. Roll out the dough on a floured work surface to about ⅛ inch thick, then cut into strips 4 inches long and ¼ inch wide.

11 Uncover the risen buns, brush the pastry strips with a little water to dampen, then arrange, sticky side down, in a cross on top of the buns.

Bake in the preheated oven for 15–20 minutes until golden brown.

12 Meanwhile, to prepare the sticky glaze, heat the milk and sugar in a small pan until dissolved, then boil for 1 minute until syrupy.

As soon as the buns are cooked, lift them out onto a cooling rack and brush immediately with the hot glaze.

Eat warm or toasted, or freeze for up to 1 month.

From the mid 1700s until 1839, the Chelsea Bun House in the fashionable Pimlico area of London made sweet, sticky fruit buns so good that even King George III lined up in the street to buy them. They were described by a diarist as flavored with honey, very sweet, and very light.

miniature chelsea buns

3 cups all-purpose flour

1 teaspoon salt, preferably sea salt

3 tablespoons light brown sugar

¾ cup tepid milk

0.6 oz. cake compressed yeast*

4 tablespoons unsalted butter, melted

1 large egg, beaten

dried fruit filling

3 tablespoons unsalted butter, melted

⅓ cup firmly packed dark brown sugar

1 cup mixed dried fruit (see note)

sweet honey glaze

3 tablespoons honey

6 tablespoons unsalted butter

5 tablespoons milk

½ cup firmly packed light brown sugar

a rectangular pan, preferably nonstick, about 13 x 9 inches, well greased

makes 24

* To use active dry yeast, mix one ¼ oz. package with the flour, salt, and sugar; then add the milk, butter, and egg. Continue as in the main recipe.

Mix the flour, salt, and sugar in a large bowl, then make a well in the center.

Put the tepid milk in a measuring cup or bowl, crumble the yeast over the top, and stir until dispersed. Pour into the well, then add the melted butter and the beaten egg. Gradually work the flour into the liquids to make a slightly soft but not sticky dough. If the dough sticks to your fingers or the bowl, work in a little more flour, 1 tablespoon at a time: if there are dry crumbs in the bowl, work in a little more tepid milk, 1 tablespoon at a time.

Turn out the dough onto a lightly floured work surface and knead thoroughly for 10 minutes until very smooth and pliable. Return the dough to the bowl, cover with plastic wrap and let rise in a warm place until doubled in size, about 1–1½ hours.

Turn out the risen dough onto a lightly floured work surface and punch down to deflate. Roll out to a rectangle about 28 x 7 inches. Brush with the melted butter, then sprinkle with the brown sugar and the dried fruit. Roll up like a jelly roll, starting with a long side and pinching the seam to seal. Using a large sharp knife, cut the roll evenly into 24 slices. Arrange them cut side up in the prepared pan so they are almost touching.

Slip the pan into a large plastic bag, inflate slightly, seal, then let rise as before until almost doubled in size, about 20–30 minutes.

Meanwhile preheat the oven to 400°F.

Put the ingredients for the glaze into a small saucepan and heat gently, stirring, until melted and smooth. Bring to the boil and simmer for about 1 minute until syrupy.

Uncover the risen buns and pour over the hot glaze. Transfer immediately to the preheated oven and bake for 15–20 minutes until golden brown. Cool in the pan for a few minutes until the glaze has firmed up but not yet set, then carefully transfer to a wire rack to cool completely. If the topping has begun to set and the buns are hard to remove from the pan, return to the oven for a few minutes to soften. Pull the buns apart when cool.

Best eaten the same or next day. Not suitable for freezing.

Note: A typical dried fruit mixture is ⅓ cup raisins, ⅓ cup dried currants, ¼ cup golden raisins, and about 2 tablespoons chopped mixed peel.

the grant loaf

If you haven't made bread before, this is the place to start. Invented accidentally by Doris Grant in England in 1944, this whole-wheat loaf has become famous for its simplicity (no kneading and just one short rising in the pan) and for its moist texture and nutty taste. The original recipe uses organic stone-ground whole-wheat flour, but I really like this loaf made with spelt flour. Not only did Mrs Grant prefer the flavor of her unusual loaf, but it cured her digestive problems—she put this down to the high Vitamin B content in unrefined flour.
A good loaf with cheeses or soups, or for sandwiches—and it makes the best breakfast toast.

step-by-step

5 cups organic stone-ground spelt flour or stone-ground whole-wheat bread flour

1 teaspoon sea salt

0.6 oz. cake compressed yeast*

1 rounded teaspoon honey

2½ cups tepid water

1 tablespoon sesame seeds, for sprinkling

a large loaf pan, 16 x 5 x 4 inches, lightly greased and gently warmed

makes 1 large loaf

* To use active dry yeast, mix one ¼ oz. package with the warmed flour and salt. Add all the tepid water and the honey, then mix and proceed as in the main recipe. Allow slightly longer for the dough to rise.

1 Put the flour and salt in a large bowl and mix well. Make a well in the center.

In cold weather, gently warm the flour in a low oven at 300°F for a few minutes. Alternatively, microwave on HIGH for 15 seconds. This will help the yeast grow and give a lighter loaf.

2 Crumble the fresh yeast into a small bowl.

3 Add the honey.

4 Add about ⅔ cup of the tepid water. Stir until smooth and creamy. Leave for 10 minutes until frothy.

5 Pour the yeast liquid and the remaining tepid water into the well in the flour.

6 The yeast liquid will become very bubbly and active.

7 Mix vigorously with your hand for 1–2 minutes, working from the sides to the center until the dough feels elastic and slippery, and comes cleanly away from the sides of the bowl. It will be much wetter than a standard bread dough.

8 Put the dough into the prepared pan and cover with a damp cloth. Leave in a warm place for about 25–35 minutes until the dough rises to within ½ inch of the top of the pan.

Meanwhile, preheat the oven to 400°F.

9 Sprinkle with the sesame seeds, then bake in the preheated oven for 35–40 minutes.

10 Using a cloth or oven gloves to protect your hands, remove the loaf from the pan and tap it underneath with your knuckles. It should sound hollow, like a drum. If it sounds heavy and dead, then return it to the oven, bake for 5 minutes more, then test again. Transfer the bread to a wire rack to cool completely.

Best eaten within 4 days or toasted. Can be frozen for up to 1 month.

A deliciously aromatic loaf, with the wonderful complex taste of German malt beer (stout, such as Guinness, is an alternative). The long rising time develops the flavor and avoids a crumbly loaf. Good with tangy cheese.

german beer bread

Crumble the yeast into a large pitcher. Add the malt syrup, honey, and beer and stir until completely dispersed.

Mix the flours and salt in a large bowl. Using the tips of your fingers, rub in the fat until the mixture looks like breadcrumbs. Make a well in the center, then pour in the yeast liquid. Gradually work the flour into the liquid to make a soft dough that feels tacky—if the dough feels wet and sticky, work in a extra white flour, 1 tablespoon at a time: if there are dry crumbs in the base of the bowl, work in a little more beer or stout, 1 tablespoon at a time.

Turn out the dough onto a lightly floured work surface and knead energetically for 10 minutes: the dough will feel firmer and far less tacky.

Return the dough to the bowl and cover tightly with plastic wrap. Let rise in a cool place very slowly until doubled in size, about 6–8 hours or overnight in the refrigerator.

Turn out on to a lightly floured work surface and punch down to deflate. Shape into a neat ball and set on the prepared tray. Slip the tray into a large plastic bag, slightly inflate, then close tightly and let rise in a warm place until doubled in size, about 1–4 hours depending on the initial temperature of the dough.

Meanwhile, preheat the oven to 400°F.

Uncover the loaf and brush lightly with beer. Sprinkle with cracked rye or wheat, then score with a sharp knife or razor blade. Bake in the preheated oven for 35 minutes or until the loaf sounds hollow when tapped underneath. Cool on a wire rack.

Best eaten within 5 days, or toasted. Can be frozen for up to 1 month.

one-third 0.6 oz. cake compressed yeast*

1 tablespoon malt syrup

1 tablespoon honey

1⅛ cups malt beer or sweet stout

2¾ cups all-purpose flour

¾ cup rye flour

⅔ cup whole-wheat bread flour

1½ teaspoons salt, preferably sea salt

2 tablespoons vegetable shortening, lard, or butter, diced

2 tablespoons beer, for brushing

cracked rye or wheat, for sprinkling

a baking sheet, greased

makes 1 large loaf

* To use easy-blend dried yeast, mix ¼ teaspoon with the flours and salt. Rub in the fat, then add the malt syrup, honey, and beer or stout. Continue as in the main recipe.

german rye bread

This makes a traditional, deeply flavored bread with close texture and good crust. It uses a sourdough starter rather than yeast and a high proportion of rye flour. For a milder, lighter loaf you could use equal quantities of rye and all-purpose flour. The flavor of this bread develops and matures after baking and keeps particularly well.

6 cups stone-ground dark rye flour

1½ cups all-purpose flour

½ cup cut rye grains,* plus extra for finishing

2 teaspoons salt, preferably sea salt

a good pinch of ground caraway seeds

1⅔ cups thick batter sourdough starter (see page 13)

about 1⅔ cups tepid water

2 baking sheets, greased

makes 2 medium loaves

* Available from natural food stores and the suppliers on page 142

1 Put the flours, cut rye grains, salt, and ground caraway seeds in large bowl, mix well, then make a well in the center. In chilly weather gently warm the flour mixture in a low oven at 300°F for a few minutes or microwave on HIGH for 15 seconds.

2 Tip the sourdough starter into the well.

3 Add the water and stir until soupy.

4 Using your hand, gradually work the flour into the liquid to make a soft dough. Flours and starters vary, so you may need to add more water, or if the dough feels very sticky, some more white flour. This dough will feel heavier and will stick to your fingers more than an all-wheat dough; it will also be harder to work.

5 Turn out the dough onto a lightly floured work surface and knead energetically for about 10 minutes.

Alternatively, use the dough hook of a free-standing mixer and work for 5 minutes on low speed.

6 Return the dough to the bowl, cover with plastic film, then let rise until doubled in size.*

Rye flour needs plenty of encouragement, so a fairly warm humid atmosphere, like a steamy kitchen, works best.

* Depending on the vigor of your starter and the room temperature, the dough can take anything from about 3–8 hours to double in size. I leave it to rise on a rack over the stove, usually overnight unless the weather is very hot.

7 Punch down the risen dough a couple of times to deflate, or turn it out onto a lightly floured work surface before punching it down.

Divide the dough into 2 equal pieces and shape each into a neat round. Roll the loaves in the extra cut rye, then set on the prepared trays.

Slip the trays into a large plastic bag, inflate gently, then fasten.

8 The shaped loaves can also be risen in canvas-lined proving baskets, or in wicker baskets or colanders lined with heavily floured linen cloths.

9 Let rise in a warm spot until doubled in size, about 3–5 hours, depending on the temperature and the vigor of your dough.

Towards the end of the rising time preheat the oven to 425°F. Put a roasting pan of water in the base of the oven to create steam.

If you have been proving the dough in a basket, put 2 unfloured baking sheets or a baking stone in the oven to heat.

10 Uncover the risen dough or swiftly turn the loaves out of their baskets onto the hot trays.

11 Slash the top of each loaf with a sharp knife or razor blade, then put into the preheated oven. If you have a water spray or mister, give the oven a good spray to add to the steamy atmosphere—this will help the dough rise in the oven (called "ovenspring").

12 Bake for about 35 minutes until the loaves sound hollow when tapped underneath.

Cool on a wire rack. For best flavor, wrap and keep overnight before slicing.

This loaf will keep for up to a week and makes good toast. Freeze for up to 1 month.

This is the well-loved, rather sturdy loaf from the Swiss canton of Valais. It is made from the local "farmer's mix," a combination of dark rye and wheat flours with the coarse, flaky texture of Irish soda or graham flour, plus milk. To get a similar taste and texture, I use a mixture of stone-ground rye and whole-wheat flour, plus graham flour. A good bread with cheese and pâté.

swiss farmer's bread

Mix the flours and salt in a large bowl—in cold weather, gently warm in a low oven or microwave. Make a well in the center.

Put the milk and water into a measuring cup or bowl, crumble the yeast over the top, and stir until dispersed. Pour into the well, then gradually work the flour into the liquid to make a slightly soft dough. Flours vary, so if the dough feels sticky, work in extra flour, 1 tablespoon at a time: if there are dry crumbs in the bowl, or the dough feels tough and dry, work in extra tepid milk or water, 1 tablespoon at a time.

Turn out into a lightly floured work surface and knead thoroughly for 5 minutes.

Return the dough to the bowl, cover with plastic wrap, then let rise in a warm place until doubled in size, about 1½–2 hours.

Turn out the dough onto a lightly floured work surface and punch down to deflate. Shape into a ball, roll in a little graham flour to coat, and set on the prepared tray. Slip the tray into a large plastic bag, inflate slightly, then let rise as before until doubled in size, about 1 hour. Don't worry if the top looks slightly cracked.

Meanwhile, preheat the oven to 450°F and set a roasting pan of water in the bottom to create a steamy atmosphere.

Uncover the loaf and, using a sharp knife or razor blade, score well in a diamond pattern. Bake in the preheated oven for 25–30 minutes until the loaf sounds hollow when tapped underneath. Cool on a wire rack.

Best eaten within 6 days or toasted. Can be frozen for up to 1 month.

1⅔ cups stone-ground dark rye flour

⅔ cup stone-ground whole-wheat bread flour

¾ cup graham flour, plus extra for rolling

¾ teaspoon salt, preferably sea salt

⅔ cup mixture of tepid milk and ⅔ cup tepid water, mixed

0.6 oz. cake compressed yeast*

a baking sheet, well greased

makes 1 medium loaf

* To use active dry yeast, mix one ¼ oz. package with the flours and salt; then work in the tepid milk mixture and continue as in the main recipe.

polish poppy seed roll

I once lived opposite a Polish deli and on Thursdays, their baking day, it was crowded with émigrés and devotees waiting for their heavenly poppy seed and rum roll. Eat cut in thick slices with a cup of the best coffee you can find.

1¾ cups all-purpose flour

¼ teaspoon salt, preferably sea salt

2 teaspoons sugar

4 tablespoons unsalted butter, diced

about ⅓ cup tepid milk

two-thirds of 0.6 oz cake compressed yeast*

1 medium egg

dried fruit and poppy seed filling

½ cup mixed dried fruit and peel (*see* note page 81)

2 tablespoons rum

¾ cup poppy seeds

¼ cup honey

to glaze

1 egg yolk

1 teaspoon confectioners' sugar

a large baking sheet, well greased

makes 1 medium loaf

* To use easy-blend dried yeast, mix half a ¼ oz. package with the flour, salt, and sugar; then rub in the butter. Add the milk and egg, and continue as in the main recipe.

If making the dough in cold weather, gently warm the flour in a low oven, 300°F, for a few minutes—this will give the yeast a flying start.

Put the flour in a large mixing bowl, then mix in the salt and sugar. Using the tips of your fingers, rub in the diced butter until the mixture looks like fine crumbs. Make a well in the center.

Put the tepid milk in a measuring cup or bowl, crumble the yeast over the top, and stir well until dispersed. Pour into the well. Mix the egg into the yeast liquid. Gradually work the flour into the liquid to make a smooth, soft dough. If the dough is dry or there are crumbs in the bowl, add more milk, 1 tablespoon at a time.

Turn out on to a lightly floured work surface and knead thoroughly for 10 minutes. Return the dough to the bowl, cover with plastic wrap, and let rise in a warm place until doubled in size, about 1½–2 hours.

Meanwhile, to make the filling, mix the dried fruit and rum in a small saucepan and let soak. Put the poppy seeds in a heatproof bowl and pour over enough boiling water to cover. Leave for 5 minutes, then drain well in a very fine strainer (or one lined with cheesecloth). Grind the seeds in a spice grinder or with a mortar and pestle. Add the honey to the soaked fruit in the pan and heat gently until melted. Add the crushed poppy seeds, then bring to a boil, stirring constantly. Remove from the heat and let cool.

Turn out the risen dough onto a floured work surface and punch down to deflate. Roll out to a rectangle about 12 x 8 inches and a little less than ½ inch thick.

Spread the filling evenly over the dough to within ½ inch of the edges. Roll up the dough from one side like a jelly roll, then tuck the ends underneath. Pinch the seam firmly to seal. Arrange on the prepared tray with the seam side underneath. Slip it into a large plastic bag, slightly inflate the bag, then let rise as before until doubled in size, about 1½ hours, or overnight in the refrigerator.

Meanwhile, preheat the oven to 375°F.

Mix the beaten egg with the confectioners' sugar, uncover the risen loaf, and brush it with the mixture. Bake in the preheated oven for about 35 minutes until firm and golden brown. Cool on a wire rack.

Eat within 4 days. Not suitable for freezing.

swedish saffron bread

Saffron flavored breads, cakes, and cookies are popular at holiday time in Sweden. This is a traditional Christmas bread, and the same dough flavored with raisins is used to make Lucia cats, the small twisted rolls eaten on St. Lucia's morning, December 13.

Crumble the saffron into a small heatproof bowl, then pour over the boiling water, cover, and let soak for as long as possible, up to 12 hours.

When ready to make the dough, put the tepid milk in a bowl or measuring cup and crumble the yeast over the top. Add the egg and beat gently.

Mix the flour, salt, and sugar in a large bowl and make a well in the center. Pour the yeast liquid, saffron liquid (scrape out every last bit), and the cooled melted butter into the well. Mix well, then gradually work in the flour to make a very smooth dough. If the dough feels sticky, work in a little more flour, 1 tablespoon at a time: if it seems dry or there are crumbs in the base of the bowl, work in extra milk or water, 1 tablespoon at a time.

Turn out the dough onto a lightly floured work surface and knead thoroughly for 5 minutes until very pliable and silky smooth.

Return the dough to the bowl, cover with plastic wrap, and let rise in a warm place until doubled in size, about 1 hour.

Turn out the risen dough onto a lightly floured work surface and punch down to deflate. Divide the dough into 7 equal pieces and shape each into a sausage about 9 inches long. Roll up the dough to make neat spirals. Set one in the center of the prepared tray. Arrange the rest of the spirals around the central one, slightly touching, with the spirals all in the same direction. Slip the tray into a large plastic bag, inflate, then fasten and let rise in a warm place until almost doubled in size, about 30 minutes.

Meanwhile, preheat the oven to 400°F.

Uncover the risen dough, then brush lightly with the beaten egg glaze. Avoid glueing the dough to the tray.

Bake in the preheated oven for about 25 minutes until golden and firm. Cool on a wire rack.

Best eaten within 2 days or toasted. Can also be frozen for up to 1 month.

Note: The risen dough can punched down and shaped into a cylinder to fit a standard loaf pan, 9 x 5 x 3 inches. Rise again until doubled in size, then bake at 350°F for about 1 hour.

½ teaspoon saffron threads

2 tablespoons boiling water

1 cup tepid milk

0.6 oz. cake compressed yeast*

1 large egg

3¼ cups all-purpose flour

1 teaspoon salt, preferably sea salt

¼ cup sugar

7 tablespoons unsalted butter, melted

1 egg, beaten, to glaze

a large baking sheet, well greased

makes 1 large loaf

* To use active dry yeast, mix one ¼ oz. package with the flour, salt, and sugar. Add the milk, saffron, and melted butter and continue as in the main recipe.

vetebrod

A sweet loaf from Sweden to serve with coffee. The rich dough is flavored with fragrant cardamom—which is a common though costly spice in Scandinavian pastries— and the filling with ground cinnamon.

To make the dough, put the butter and milk in a measuring cup or bowl and leave until the butter has melted and the liquid is tepid. Crumble the yeast into the liquid and stir until thoroughly dispersed.

Mix the flour, salt, and sugar in a large bowl. Remove the black seeds from the cardamom pods, crush to a fine powder using a mortar and pestle, then add to the flour. Make a well in the center of the flour and pour in the yeast liquid. Gradually work the flour into the liquid to make a soft but not sticky dough. If the dough feels sticky, work in a little more flour, 1 tablespoon at a time: if there are dry crumbs in the bowl, or the dough feels dry, work in a little more milk or water, 1 tablespoon at a time.

Turn out the dough onto a lightly floured work surface and knead thoroughly for 10 minutes until smooth, silky, and very elastic. Return the dough to the bowl, cover with plastic wrap, then let rise in a warm place until doubled in size, about 1 hour.

Meanwhile, put the filling ingredients in a bowl and beat until soft and creamy.

Turn out the risen dough onto a lightly floured work surface and punch down to deflate. Roll out to a 12-inch square. Spread the filling evenly over the surface, then roll up lengthwise like a jelly roll. Pinch the seam well to seal, then put onto the prepared tray with the seam underneath. Using kitchen shears, snip the roll almost all the way through at ½-inch intervals, then pull the snipped pieces to left and right alternately. Slip the tray into a large plastic bag, seal, and inflate slightly, then let rise as before until doubled in size, about 45 minutes–1 hour.

Meanwhile preheat the oven to 400°F.

Uncover the dough and bake in the preheated oven for 20 minutes until firm and golden. Remove from the tray to a wire rack, cover with a dry cloth, and let cool.

Serve dusted with confectioners' sugar, or sprinkle with pearl sugar before baking.

Best eaten the same day or within 3 days. Can be frozen for up to 1 month.

4 tablespoons unsalted butter, softened and diced

⅔ cup hot milk

0.6 oz. cake compressed yeast*

2 cups all-purpose flour

½ teaspoon salt, preferably sea salt

¼ cup light brown sugar

10 green cardamom pods

confectioners' sugar or pearl sugar*, to serve

cinnamon filling

4 tablespoons unsalted butter, softened

4 tablespoons light brown sugar

1 teaspoon ground cinnamon

a large baking sheet, well greased

makes 1 medium loaf

* To use active dry yeast, mix one ¼ oz. package with the flour, salt, sugar, and cardamom. Add the melted butter and milk and continue as in the main recipe.

** See mail order, page 142

africa and the middle east

Leavened bread was probably first made in ancient Egypt, and archaeological studies indicate that little has changed in the way bread has been made in this part of the world since. The breads of the region are immune to fashion.

Quickly baked flatbreads—round, oval, or large scarf-like sheets—appear at almost every meal. They are made from a variety of grains, ranging from wheat to millet, leavened with yeast or a saved-dough starter, and often flavored with herbs or spices. The best-known is the ubiquitous pita bread, found in almost every takeout lunch bar from New York to London, from Seattle to Sydney. On its home ground, it is used instead of cutlery or plates, and eaten with mezze, the Middle Eastern version of tapas or antipasti. According to *The Oxford Companion to Food*, the mezze tradition, originally from Persia, extends westward from Turkey into the Balkans and Greece and southward through Lebanon, Egypt, and North Africa to Morocco. Wherever they are eaten, mezze are accompanied by bread.

Not all breads are flatbreads however, as can be seen in the markets and souks throughout the region, with women and children taking great trays of unbaked loaves to the local communal baker for cooking, then taking them home again, fragrant and ready to eat.

kahk

Kahk are Arab bread bracelets or rings. In this Iraqi recipe, they are flavored with roasted cumin and coriander, then brushed with egg and coated with sesame seeds. Other recipes call for black onion seeds (nigella) or fenugreek, while allspice and chile are popular in Morocco. Kahk are eaten as part of a mezze or as a snack.

2 cups all-purpose flour

1 teaspoon salt, preferably sea salt

2 teaspoons cumin seeds, roasted*

1 teaspoon coriander seeds, roasted and ground*

0.6 oz. cake compressed yeast**

scant ½ cup tepid water

scant ½ cup olive oil

1 egg, beaten, to glaze

sesame seeds, to sprinkle

several baking sheets, well greased

makes 18

* To roast whole spices— put the spices, one kind at a time, in a small, heavy, ungreased skillet. Stir over medium heat for a couple of minutes until they start to smell fragrant and turn slightly darker in color.

** To use active dry yeast, mix one ¼ oz. package with the flour and spices, then add the water and oil, and proceed as in the main recipe.

Put the flour, salt, and roasted whole and ground spices in a large bowl and mix well. Make a well in the center.

Crumble the yeast into a small bowl, add the water, stir until dispersed, then pour into the well, together with the olive oil. Gradually draw the flour into the liquids to make a firm, heavy dough. If the dough feels sticky, work in a little more flour, 1 tablespoon at a time: if there are dry crumbs in the bowl, work in a little more tepid water, 1 tablespoon at a time.

Turn out onto a lightly floured work surface and knead thoroughly for 10 minutes. Return the dough to the bowl, cover with plastic wrap, and leave in a warm place until doubled in size, about 1½ hours.

Turn out the risen dough onto a lightly floured work surface and punch down to deflate. Divide into 18 equal pieces about the size of a walnut. Using your hands, roll the pieces into sausages about 5 inches long. Join the ends to form rings.

Arrange slightly apart on the prepared baking sheets, then very lightly brush with beaten egg, taking care not to glue the dough to the trays. Sprinkle with sesame seeds. Slip the trays into large plastic bags, slightly inflate, seal, then let rise as before until doubled in size, about 30 minutes.

Meanwhile, preheat the oven to 375°F.

Uncover the rings and bake for 25 minutes until firm and golden. Remove from the oven, turn down the heat to its lowest setting, then, when the oven has cooled sufficiently, bake for a further 20 minutes until crisp and dry. Cool on a wire rack.

Eat immediately or store in an airtight container for up to 1 month.

Another popular hot snack from Turkey. A very thin, pizza-like base is covered with a spicy meat mixture and quickly baked. As soon as it comes out of the oven it is rolled up and eaten with the fingers.

lahmacun
turkish flatbread wraps

3 cups all-purpose flour

1½ teaspoons salt, preferably sea salt

0.6 oz. cake compressed yeast*

1¼ cups tepid water

1 tablespoon virgin olive oil

spicy meat topping

9 oz. very lean ground beef or lamb

1 small onion, very finely chopped

1 tomato, peeled, seeded, and finely chopped

1 red chile (or to taste), seeded and finely chopped, or ½ red bell pepper, seeded and finely chopped

1 heaped tablespoon chopped fresh flat-leaf parsley or cilantro

salt, preferably sea salt, and freshly ground black pepper

2 tablespoons virgin olive oil

4 large baking sheets, greased

makes 4 large breads

* To use active dry yeast, mix one ¼ oz. package with the flour and salt. Add all the water and oil and mix to make a soft dough, omitting the sponge stage.

To make the dough, mix the flour and salt in a large bowl. Make a well in the center, then crumble in the yeast. Pour in the water and stir to disperse the yeast. Mix in the oil, then gradually draw in enough of the flour to make a thick batter. Cover the bowl with a dry cloth and leave for about 20 minutes until puffed and sponge-like. Work in the rest of the flour to make a soft but not sticky dough. If the dough feels sticky, then work in a little more flour, 1 tablespoon at a time: if the dough is dry and crumbly, add a little more water, 1 tablespoon at a time.

Turn out the dough onto a lightly floured work surface and knead thoroughly for 10 minutes. Return the dough to the bowl, cover with plastic wrap, and let rise in a warm place until doubled in size, about 1 hour.

Turn out the risen dough onto a floured work surface and punch down to deflate. Divide the dough into 4 equal pieces and let rest for 5 minutes while preparing the topping. Preheat the oven to 400°F.

Put all the topping ingredients, except the olive oil, in a bowl and mix well.

Roll out the dough as thinly as possible, about 1⁄16 inch, to make 4 large disks or rectangles to fit your baking sheets. Try to keep the rim of the dough thin—if necessary trim off the edges with a sharp knife.

Set the thin sheets of dough on the prepared trays, then brush lightly with olive oil. Sprinkle with the meat topping, breaking up any clumps of meat—the topping is not intended to cover the dough, but to add flavor. Transfer immediately to the preheated oven and bake until firm and lightly browned, about 12 minutes. Remove from the oven and quickly and carefully roll up or fold over the dough. Wrap in a paper napkin and eat immediately.

cilantro and olive pita breads

Round or oval, plain or flavored, pita breads have found a niche in our supermarkets and restaurants. Easily split and filled with falafel and salad, or cut into wedges and used to eat dips and mezze dishes, pitas are interesting to make. They puff up like balloons in the oven—it's fun to watch.

1¼ cups tepid water

0.6 oz. cake compressed yeast*

1½ tablespoons virgin olive oil

about 3¼ cups all-purpose flour

2 teaspoons sea salt

2½ tablespoons chopped cilantro leaves

a good pinch of ground cumin

½ cup good quality black olives, such as kalamata or niçoise, pitted and chopped

several baking sheets

makes 12 large breads

* To use active dry yeast, mix one ¼ oz. package with the flour in Step 2, then work into the water and oil, adding the salt with the second addition.

1 Put the water in a small bowl, crumble the yeast over the top, and stir until dispersed.

2 Pour the virgin olive oil into the bowl and mix well.

3 Add a handful of the flour to the yeast mixture and beat with your hand to make a smooth batter. Add another handful of the flour and the salt and work in. Add the remaining flour, a handful at a time, working the dough well as it forms into a soft but not sticky dough.

4 Turn out the dough onto a floured work surface, cover with the upturned bowl, and let rest for 5 minutes.

5 Knead the dough energetically for 5 minutes, until very supple and smooth.

6 Flatten into a disk and sprinkle with the cilantro, cumin, and olives.

7 Knead the flavorings into the dough until evenly distributed, about 3–4 minutes.

8 Return the dough to the bowl, cover with plastic wrap, and let rise in a warm place until doubled in size, about 1 hour.

Turn out the risen dough onto a lightly floured work surface, punch down with your knuckles and divide into 12 equal pieces. Shape each into a ball, then cover with plastic wrap or a dry cloth and let rest for about 10 minutes.

9 With a lightly floured rolling pin, roll out each ball to a circle or slightly oval shape about 6 inches across and ¼ inch thick.

10 Arrange the breads in a single layer on a well-floured dry cloth and let rise until doubled in size, about 30 minutes.

Meanwhile, preheat your oven to its maximum setting and put a baking stone or well-used baking sheet into the oven to heat.

11 Bake the pita breads in batches. Protect your hands with thick oven gloves or cloth and quickly transfer the batch of breads to the hot baking stone or sheet. Lightly splash or spray them with water, then bake for 2 minutes.

12 Check the breads are not browning too much, then cook for another minute or so, depending on the heat of your oven. If the breads brown too much before they are firm, lower the heat slightly. Remove from the oven as soon as they are firm.

Transfer to a wire rack to cool slightly, then cover with a dry cloth to keep the crust soft.

Eat warm or lightly broiled as soon as possible after baking. Can be frozen for up to 1 month. Warm through before eating.

This Turkish snack, *pide*, is a rich, cheese-flavored cross between a quiche and a pizza—from my good friend Zeynep Conker Stromfelt, whose mother is a well-known cook in Istanbul, famous for her bread and pastries.

peynirli pide

To make the dough, put the flour into a large bowl and make a well in the center. Crumble the yeast into the well, then add the water and stir until the yeast has dispersed. Work in enough of the flour to make a very thick batter. Cover the bowl with a dry cloth and leave for 15 minutes or until the yeast mixture looks puffed and sponge-like. Add the milk and eggs to the yeast mixture, then work in the flour and salt to make a soft dough.

Turn out onto a floured work surface and knead thoroughly for 5 minutes. Work in the soft butter and knead again for 1 minute until evenly distributed. Return the dough to the bowl, cover with plastic wrap, and let rise in a warm place until doubled in size, about 1½ hours.

Turn out the dough onto a floured work surface and punch down to deflate. Divide the dough into 6 equal pieces and shape into balls using well-floured hands. Pat or roll out the balls to ovals, about 6 inches long. Pinch and crimp the rim of each oval to prevent the filling spilling over the edge. Arrange well apart on the prepared trays.

To make the filling, put all the ingredients in a bowl and mix with a fork. Spread the filling in the center of each oval then dot with little flakes of butter. Let rise for about 20–30 minutes.

Meanwhile, preheat the oven to 400°F.

Transfer the baking sheets to the preheated oven and bake for 20 minutes. Eat while still warm.

2½ cups all-purpose flour

0.6 oz. cake compressed yeast*

3 tablespoons tepid water

scant ½ cup tepid milk

2 large eggs, beaten

1 teaspoon salt, preferably sea salt

2 tablespoons unsalted butter, very soft

cheese filling

6 oz. feta cheese, crumbled

1 large egg, beaten

several grinds of black pepper

1 rounded tablespoon chopped, flat-leaf parsley

several dashes of Tabasco sauce

about 1½ tablespoons butter, for dotting

several baking sheets, greased

makes 6 large pides

* To use active dry yeast, mix one ¼ oz. package with the flour. Add the water, milk, and eggs and make the dough, omitting the initial sponge stage.

North Africa is one of the world's great orange-growing regions and delicious orange flower water is one of the great flavors of Arab cooking. It gives these rich, quite sweet rolls a taste of Algeria. They are lovely for breakfast.

mounas

Mix the flour, salt, and sugar in a large bowl. Make a well in the center and crumble in the yeast. Add the water and stir to disperse the yeast. Work in a little of the flour to make a thick batter. Cover the bowl with a dry cloth and leave for 20 minutes until puffed and spongy.

Add the beaten eggs, orange zest, olive oil, and orange flower water to the sponge mixture and stir well. Gradually draw in the flour to make a soft and slightly sticky dough. If the dough feels too sticky, work in a little more flour, 1 tablespoon at a time: if there are dry crumbs in the bowl, work in a little more tepid water, 1 tablespoon at a time.

Turn out onto a lightly floured work surface and knead thoroughly for 10 minutes. Return the dough to the bowl, cover with plastic wrap, and let rise until doubled in size—the dough is very heavy, so allow about 3 hours in a warm room or overnight in a cooler place.

Turn out the dough onto a floured work surface and punch down to deflate. Divide the dough into 12 equal pieces. Shape each into a ball and set, well apart, on the prepared trays. Slip the trays into a large plastic bag, inflate, seal, and let rise until doubled in size, about 1 hour in a warm place.

Meanwhile, preheat the oven to 400°F.

Uncover the dough, lightly brush with the egg glaze, and bake in the preheated oven for about 15 minutes until golden brown and firm. Cool on a wire rack. Dust with confectioners' sugar and eat warm with coffee the same day.

3 cups all-purpose flour

1 teaspoon salt, preferably sea salt

½ cup sugar

0.6 oz. cake compressed yeast*

½ cup tepid water

2 large eggs, beaten

the grated zest of I orange, organic or unwaxed

3 tablespoons virgin olive oil

2 tablespoons orange flower water

beaten egg, to glaze

confectioners' sugar, for dusting

2 baking sheets, well greased

makes 12

* To use active dry yeast, mix one ¼ oz. package with ⅔ cup of the flour. Work in the water to make a thick batter, then leave for 20 minutes. Add the eggs, orange zest, oil, and orange flower water, then work in the rest of the flour mixed with the salt and sugar.

Turkestan is part of the former Soviet Union, adjoining Iran and Afghanistan, and since Biblical times has been the home of the nomadic Turkmen tribes. Their favorite bread is bursting with toasted seeds and nuts and has traveled with them wherever they have settled. I've added bakers' yeast to the traditional sourdough starter to improve the texture of the baked loaf. Good with soup and salads.

turkestan loaf

Mix the flour, salt, seeds, cracked rye and wheat, and the spelt or wheat flakes in a large bowl. Make a well in the center.

Crumble the yeast into a small bowl, add the honey and half the water, and stir until dispersed. Pour into the well, along with the rest of the water and the sourdough starter. Stir the liquids together, then gradually draw in the dry ingredients to make a soft but not sticky dough. If the dough sticks to your fingers, work in a little more flour, 1 tablespoon at a time: if it feels hard and dry, work in a bit more water, 1 tablespoon at a time—the amount of liquid needed will depend on the thickness of the starter.

Turn out the dough onto a lightly floured work surface and knead thoroughly for 10 minutes. Return the dough to the bowl, then put the bowl into a large plastic bag or cover with plastic wrap. Leave in a warm place to rise until doubled in size, about 2 hours.

Turn out the risen dough onto a lightly floured work surface and gradually work in the nuts. Shape the dough into a ball and set on the baking sheet. Cover and let rise as before until the dough has doubled in size, about 1 hour.

Meanwhile, preheat the oven to 425°F.

Uncover the risen loaf, transfer the baking sheet to the preheated oven, and bake for about 35 minutes or until the loaf sounds hollow when tapped underneath. Cool on a wire rack.

Best eaten within 4 days or toasted. Can be frozen for up to 1 month.

3½ cups organic stone-ground spelt or whole-wheat flour

2 teaspoons salt, preferably sea salt

2 tablespoon sunflower seeds

2 tablespoons sesame seeds

1 tablespoon flaxseeds

1 tablespoon pumpkin seeds

2½ tablespoons cracked rye

2½ tablespoons cracked wheat

⅓ cup spelt or wheat flakes

0.6 oz. cake compressed yeast*

1 tablespoon honey

1⅓ cups tepid water

1 cup sourdough starter (page 13)

⅓ cup toasted walnut halves, coarsely chopped

⅓ cup toasted almonds, coarsely chopped

⅓ cup toasted hazelnuts, coarsely chopped

a baking sheet, greased

makes 1 large loaf

* To use active dry yeast in place of the fresh yeast and sourdough starter, mix 1½ packages (¼ oz. each) with the flour and salt. Mix in the seeds, cracked wheat, and rye, and the wheat flakes. Make a well in the center, add the honey, and the tepid water, then continue as in the main recipe.

south asia

Civilization has flourished in South Asia for at least 5000 years and there is archaeological evidence that wheat and barley were early staples in some parts. Even though the Subcontinent is so vast—with a huge range of climatic, geographical and agricultural conditions and a massive, diverse population—meals throughout are based on cereals. Rice or bread, along with vegetables and pulses flavored with spices, are essential.

Wheat breads are made every day in homes in Northern India and Pakistan. Roti, also known as chapatti, is also the word for "bread" across the Indian Subcontinent. Made from a very finely milled whole-wheat flour known as atta, the yeastless dough is rolled out very thinly, then quickly cooked on a heavy dry iron tawa or griddle. It is used immediately as an edible scoop. Tandoor ovens, made from clay and sunk into the ground, have spread from the Punjab throughout the Subcontinent. Traditionally, women would bring ready made bread dough to the communal ovens. There they would chat, shape, and rapidly bake the many naan needed for large extended families.

Further south, where wheat is not grown, lentils, pulses, and rice are staples. These are ground and fermented to make batters for feather-light but sturdy pancakes, eaten as a wrapping or a scoop.

Now that authentic ingredients are more readily available around the world, we can now try to reproduce the time-honored, wondrous dishes of the Subcontinent, in the way they have traditionally been eaten, with bread.

pooris

Pooris are disks of dough fried in hot oil rather than cooked on a dry skillet. Serve hot with spicy curries of vegetables, lentils, or meat. Tiny poori, about 2 inches across, are the perfect snack with a beer. Just pull off marble-sized pieces of the dough, then pat out and fry as below.

1¾ cups atta (chapatti) flour or all-purpose flour

1 teaspoon salt

1 teaspoon cumin seeds

1 teaspoon coriander seeds

1 teaspoon black peppercorns

1 tablespoon melted ghee or clarified butter

2 tablespoons yogurt

about generous ½ cup cold water

vegetable oil, for frying

a wok, karahi (Indian wok), deep skillet, or deep-fryer

makes 12

Mix the flour and salt in a large bowl. Put the cumin, coriander, and peppercorns in a small skillet and stir-fry over medium heat for 2–3 minutes until aromatic and the cumin is golden brown. Crush to a coarse powder with a spice mill or mortar and pestle. Stir into the flour. Sprinkle the melted ghee or butter over the mixture and work in with your fingers.

Mix the yogurt with half the water, then add to the dough and mix until flakes of dough start to come together. Gradually add enough of the remaining water to make a stiff dough that holds together. Using unfloured hands, knead and work the dough in the bowl until it feels smooth and pliable. Wrap the dough in plastic wrap and let it rest for at least 15 minutes or up to 2 hours, at most.

On an unfloured work surface, divide the dough into 12 equal pieces. Shape them into balls by rolling them between your palms.

Flatten each ball into a disk with a lump in the middle by rotating the dough between the palm of one hand and the fingers of the other, using your fingers to press and gently pull out the rim. Use a rolling pin to make a neat disk about 5 inches across. As you get used to this, the dough will rotate as you roll, but to begin with you will need to keep turning it yourself. Roll out the remaining dough and let rest on a lightly floured tray or work surface, covered with a dry cloth.

Meanwhile, heat about 1 inch of oil in the wok, karahi, skillet, or deep-fryer. When the oil reaches 350°F, or when a small cube of bread will brown in 40 seconds, carefully slip 1 poori into the oil. When it puffs up, turn it over with a slotted spoon. Spoon some oil over the top and turn it over again. The

poori will puff up like an over-stuffed cushion and be lightly speckled with brown—it will be cooked in about a minute. Remove with a slotted spoon and drain on a couple of sheets of paper towels. Cook the rest in the same way. Serve the pooris immediately.

Potato Sesame Pooris Using a fork or potato ricer, mash 5 oz. boiled potatoes until very smooth and lump-free (do not use a food processor or you will have wallpaper paste).

Let cool, then work in 1 cup atta flour or all-purpose flour, 1 teaspoon salt, and 1 tablespoon sesame seeds. Mix to make a firm dough. If the dough is dry and won't come together, work in a little water, about 1 tablespoon at a time.

Work and knead the dough in the bowl or on an unfloured work surface for 5 minutes until very smooth. Wrap and let rest for at least 15 minutes or up to 2 hours. Divide the dough into 8 equal pieces, then roll out to paper-thin disks, 5 inches in diameter.

Heat the oil as in the main recipe and cook the potato pooris in the same way. Drain well on paper towels and eat warm as soon as possible.

dosa

The dosa—a thin pancake made from a fermented batter of rice and dhaal (lentils)—is the most famous of the South Indian flatbreads and is as important there as pasta is in Italy. Unfilled dosa are eaten with a fresh, moist, coconut chutney for breakfast; a filling, usually based on potatoes, is added for a light meal. Making the batter takes time, but is quite simple with a food processor.

scant ¾ cup basmati rice

scant ½ cup urid dhaal (white Indian lentils without skins)*

¼ teaspoon salt, preferably sea salt

1 teaspoon ground cumin

peanut or sunflower oil, for greasing

makes about 10, serves 4–6

* Available from natural food stores and Indian markets.

The day before

Start the batter the day before serving. Parboil the rice until still firm in the center, about 4–5 minutes. Drain well, then let cool. Put into a measuring cup to calculate its volume, then tip into a large bowl. Stir in twice its volume of cold water (about 3 cups), cover, and let soak overnight.

Put the dhaal into another bowl, cover with 1 cup cold water, and let soak overnight.

1 Next morning, drain the rice. Put it into a food processor and blend for 1 minute. Slowly add ½ cup cold water to make a smooth paste.

2 Tip out the rice batter into a large bowl.

3 Rinse out the processor bowl, then add the drained dhaal and process as before, adding about 2–5 tablespoons cold water to make a smooth paste.

4 Add to the rice batter and stir.

5 Add the salt and cumin, then cover the bowl with a dry cloth and let ferment at room temperature for about 12 hours. The batter is well fermented when it has become a mass of bubbles.

6 When ready to cook, stir in enough water to make a medium-thick pouring consistency, like pancake or Yorkshire pudding batter.

masala dosa

with spicy potatoes and spinach

spicy potato filling

2 tablespoons ghee (clarified butter) or peanut oil

2 teaspoons black mustard seeds

2 teaspoons cumin seeds

1 medium-hot green chile, such as serrano, or to taste, seeded and thinly sliced

a good pinch of ground turmeric

½ teaspoon ground coriander

½ teaspoon ground cumin

1 lb. large baking potatoes, peeled and cut into ½-inch dice

4 cups trimmed spinach leaves

salt, to taste

7 Heat a heavy cast-iron flat griddle pan, nonstick skillet, or pancake pan until very hot. Lightly grease with half an onion or a piece of paper towel dipped in oil.

Pour a spoonful of batter onto the hot surface, then use the back of the spoon to spread it with a thin spiral motion. Home-style dosa are thick and the size of bread plates: restaurant ones are paper-thin and larger than a dinner plate. Brush a little extra oil onto the edges of the dosa, and cook until the base is crisp and golden.

8 Using a long, flexible spatula, lift off the dosa, then quickly roll. Serve dosa as soon as they are made.

Note: If the dosa is thick, flip it over and cook the other side for a couple of minutes more.

To make the filling, heat the oil in a large, heavy skillet with a lid. Add the whole spices and cook for 1 minute until the mustard seeds start to pop. Stir in the fresh chile and the ground spices and stir for 1 minute. Add the potatoes to the skillet. Stir well to coat in the spices; then lower the heat, cover with the lid, and cook gently, stirring frequently, until the potatoes are tender, about 15 minutes.

Meanwhile, rinse the spinach and shake off the excess water; then put into a large dry saucepan and cook, stirring frequently, in its own steam over medium heat until wilted. Drain thoroughly then chop coarsely.

Uncover the potatoes and turn up the heat. Stirring frequently, cook for a few minutes until starting to brown, then stir in the spinach and salt to taste. Heat through before using to fill the dosa.

naan

Naan is the most common bread in North India and Pakistan, especially the Punjab. On its home turf, it is baked in the ferociously hot, vertical clay ovens called tandoors—slapped against the sides with cloth pads, then flipped off moments later with long metal hooks. This extreme heat is impossible to match in a domestic oven, so heat your broiler to its top setting. In India, naan bread is used instead of forks or spoons, to wrap around other foods, especially grilled kebabs.

1¾ cups unbleached self-rising flour, or all-purpose flour plus 2 teaspoons baking powder

1 teaspoon salt

2 tablespoons plain yogurt

about ½ cup tepid water

melted ghee or butter, for brushing

your choice of:

1 tablespoon black onion seeds (nigella) or cumin seeds

8 garlic cloves, finely sliced

2 medium-hot red chiles such as serranos, finely sliced, seeded if preferred

1 teaspoon roasted coriander seeds, coarsely cracked, mixed with 2 tablespoons chopped fresh cilantro leaves

makes 8

Mix the flour and salt in a bowl. Add the yogurt, then gradually work in the water, using your hands, to make a soft, slightly sticky dough. Knead the dough in the bowl for a few seconds until smooth, then cover the bowl with plastic wrap and let rest for 1 hour.

When ready to cook, heat the broiler to its highest setting (see the manufacturer's instructions), then heat the broiler pan.

Divide the dough into 8 equal pieces and shape each into a ball. Using a lightly floured rolling pin, roll out each piece to an oval about 8 inches long and almost ½ inch thick. Brush the surface very lightly with melted ghee or butter, then press your choice of toppings firmly into the dough.

Put the naan on the hot broiler pan, in batches if necessary, and cook for about 30 seconds until puffy and speckled with brown spots. Carefully turn over and cook the second side for 20–30 seconds, watching constantly. Remove, brush lightly with melted ghee or butter, then serve warm as soon as possible.

roti

Roti means "bread" all across the Subcontinent. This thin, quickly prepared yeast-free bread is made with atta, a very finely milled whole-wheat flour (also known as chapatti flour), water, salt, and a little oil or ghee. Fine whole-wheat pastry flour is a good alternative. The rolled out dough is cooked on a very heavy, dry griddle or tawa and eaten immediately. Look out for *roti canai* on the streets of Malaysia, large roti in the Caribbean (introduced by Indian workers), the *rumali roti* of India made paper-thin by tossing and spinning the dough in the air, or *makkai roti* from the Punjab, made from fresh corn and cornmeal. The Sri Lankan breads made with coconut are especially good. This recipe is based on one by Charmaine Solomon.

3 cups atta flour, fine whole-wheat pastry flour or all-purpose

2 teaspoons salt, preferably sea salt

1 teaspoon baking powder

1 cup unsweetened desiccated coconut

3 tablespoons unsalted butter, diced

1 small onion

1 medium-hot fresh red chile, such as serrano, or to taste, seeded

1 large egg, beaten

melted ghee, butter, or oil, for greasing

makes 12

Mix the flour, salt, baking powder, and coconut in a large bowl. Using the tips of your fingers, rub the diced butter into the flour until the mixture looks like fine crumbs.

Finely chop the onion and chile with a sharp knife or in a food processor, then stir into the flour mixture. Add the egg and stir in with a round-bladed knife. Gradually work in about ¾ cup cold water, or enough to make a soft dough.

Wrap in plastic wrap and set aside on the work surface for 45 minutes–1 hour until ready to cook.

Divide the dough into 12 equal pieces. Put 1 piece on a floured work surface and, using your hands or a rolling pin, flatten and pat out the dough to a thin disk about 6 inches in diameter. Repeat with the other pieces of dough.

Heat a flat-surfaced griddle or a very heavy skillet, preferably cast-iron, over medium heat. If necessary, grease very lightly with half an onion dipped in the melted butter, ghee, or oil.

Cook the roti, one at a time, for 1–2 minutes on each side or until light golden brown. Keep them warm and serve hot, as soon as possible.

australia and new zealand

Like North America, Australia and New Zealand owe their wealth of diverse cultures to their immigrants. The first arrivals, from England, Scotland, and Ireland, also brought along their great farming and baking traditions. Their diet was dominated by British-style tea, bread, and jam, plus plenty of meat. A local bread, called damper, now found in the bread baskets of the trendiest restaurants, was once subsistence food—flour and water paste baked in or over campfires by drovers, stockmen, swagmen, and pioneer women.

After World War II the food map was changed forever. Australia was a haven for people from all over Europe, especially Italy and Greece, and their breads invaded Antipodean kitchens. Italians settled up and down the east coast and in the fertile Riverina region, bringing their vibrant ingredients and exciting food traditions, as well as ciabatta, focaccia, and other Italian breads. Jewish immigrants from Poland, Hungary, and Eastern Europe transformed the bakeries of Sydney and Melbourne: visit Ackland Street, St. Kilda, for instance, and you might think yourself in Old Vienna. More recently, Asian cooks have transformed Antipodean food even more, with splendid French bakeries, often run by Vietnamese bakers, producing excellent baguettes. Australia and New Zealand "have it all," as they say—the people, the food, the climate.

A great-looking, delicious, healthy bread with a moist, open texture—very popular with health-conscious young Australians and New Zealanders.

zucchini and carrot bread

Coarsely grate the zucchini into a colander. Sprinkle with 1 tablespoon of the salt, then toss the mixture so it is evenly distributed. Set the colander over a plate or bowl and leave for 20 minutes. Take small handfuls of the zucchini and squeeze well to remove all the excess water: this will prevent the dough from being too soggy.

Mix the grated carrots with the flours and remaining salt. Mix in the zucchini.

Crumble the yeast into a small bowl, add half the water, and stir until dispersed. Pour into the flour mixture and start to work the ingredients together, gradually adding as much of the remaining water as you need to make a slightly soft, untidy looking dough. Turn out onto a floured work surface and knead thoroughly for about 5 minutes until very pliable.

Return the dough to the bowl, cover with plastic wrap, and let rise in a warm place until doubled in size, about 1½ hours.

Turn out the risen dough onto a floured work surface and punch down to deflate. Divide the dough into 2 equal pieces and shape each into a cylinder to fit your pans. Set a piece of dough in each pan, then slip the pans into a large plastic bag, inflate, seal, and let rise as before until doubled in size, about 1 hour.

Meanwhile, preheat the oven to 425°F.

Brush the tops of the risen loaves with oil. Bake in the preheated oven for about 35 minutes until they are lightly browned and sound hollow when tapped underneath. Cool on a wire rack.

Best eaten within 4 days or lightly toasted. These loaves don't freeze very well.

1 lb. trimmed zucchini

1½ tablespoons salt, preferably sea salt

7 oz. trimmed carrots, peeled and coarsely grated

2⅓ cups all-purpose flour

2⅓ cups stone-ground whole-wheat flour

0.6 oz. cake compressed yeast*

1½ cups tepid water

olive oil, for brushing

2 large loaf pans, 16 x 5 x 4 inches, well greased

makes 2 large loaves

* To use active dry yeast, mix one ¼ oz. package with the flour and salt. Mix in the vegetables, then gradually work in enough water to make a slightly soft dough.

If you enjoy a loaf with plenty of texture as well as flavor, then try this. Whole wheat berries are soaked and left to sprout for a couple of days, then coarsely chopped in a processor and added to stone-ground whole-wheat and white bread flours. The dough is very lively and gives quite an open-textured and moist loaf. Because flours vary so much, and the sprouted mixture can be quite moist, it is difficult to predict the exact quantity of water needed.

sprouted wheaten bread

Rinse the whole wheat berries, put in a large bowl, and cover with cold water to about 2 inches above the surface of the berries. Soak for 24 hours. Drain well, put into a large glass jar or similar container and cover with cheesecloth. Leave in a cool, shaded place until the berries sprout and look quite hairy, about 2–3 days. Rinse and drain thoroughly, then transfer to a food processor and chop to the consistency of coarse oatmeal.

Mix the flours and salt in a large bowl. Stir in the thick, sticky, chopped berries. Crumble the yeast into a small bowl, add half the water, and stir until dispersed. Pour into the mixing bowl, then add the remaining water. Mix to make a soft dough, adding more water as necessary. If the dough feels very sticky, work in a little more flour, 1 tablespoon at a time: if there are dry crumbs in the bowl, work in a little more tepid water, 1 tablespoon at a time.

Turn out onto a lightly floured work surface and knead thoroughly for 10 minutes until the dough feels very elastic and firm.

Return the dough to the bowl, cover with plastic wrap, and leave at normal room temperature until doubled in size, about 1½ hours.

Turn out the risen dough onto a lightly floured work surface and punch down to deflate. Divide into 2 equal pieces, shape into cylinders to fit your pans, then arrange neatly in the prepared pans. Slip the pans into a large plastic bag, slightly inflated, seal, and let rise as before until almost doubled in size, about 50 minutes.

Meanwhile, preheat the oven to 425°F.

Uncover the loaves and bake in the preheated oven for 30–35 minutes or until they turn a good golden brown and sound hollow when tapped underneath. Cool on a wire rack.

The bread is best left for 12 hours before eating, and can be kept for up to 5 days. It is excellent toasted. Can be frozen for up to 1 month.

1 cup whole wheat berries

1¾ cups stone-ground whole-wheat flour

1¾ cups all-purpose flour

2 teaspoons salt, preferably sea salt

0.6 oz. cake compressed yeast*

about ¾ cup tepid water

2 standard loaf pans, 9 x 5 x 3 inches, greased

makes 2 medium loaves

* To use active dry yeast, mix one ¼ oz. package with the flours and salt, then add the processed berries and ⅔ cup of the tepid water. Mix and finish as in the main recipe.

Bread made with a good proportion of cooled mashed potatoes has wonderful flavor, excellent light texture, and lots of nutritional value. Popular with Irish, Polish, Spanish, and Russian settlers in America, Australia, and New Zealand, this bread is well worth adding to your repertoire. It's important to use baking potatoes in the ratio of four parts flour (white or whole-wheat) to one part mashed potato. For a sweet breakfast bread, Spanish style, add ⅓ cup sugar to the flour at the same time as the salt.

potato bread rolls

Put the flour into a large mixing bowl, add the diced butter, and rub in with the tips of your fingers until the mixture looks like fine crumbs. Stir in the salt and potatoes.

Put the tepid milk into a measuring cup or bowl, crumble the yeast over the top, and stir until dispersed. Pour onto the flour mixture and mix to make a firm dough.

Turn out onto a floured work surface and knead thoroughly for 10 minutes. Return the dough to the bowl, cover with plastic wrap, and let rise in a warm place until doubled in size, about 1½ hours.

Turn out the risen dough and punch down to deflate. Divide the dough into 18 equal pieces. Arrange on the prepared baking sheets, then slip them into 2 large plastic bags, and let rise as before until doubled in size, about 30 minutes.

Meanwhile, preheat the oven to 425°F.

Uncover the loaves and bake in the preheated oven for 15–20 minutes or until the turned out loaves sound hollow when tapped underneath. Cool on a wire rack.

Best eaten within 4 days, and excellent toasted. Can be frozen for up to 1 month.

5¾ cups all-purpose flour

4 tablespoons unsalted butter, diced

1 tablespoon salt, preferably sea salt

1 cup cooled mashed potatoes

1⅔ cups tepid milk

0.6 oz. cake compressed yeast*

2 baking sheets, greased

makes 18 rolls

* To use active dry yeast, mix one ¼ oz. package with the flour, then rub in the butter, mix in the salt and potato, and bind to a dough with the milk.

White bread dough is spiked with hot red pepper flakes, then filled with sharp, mature, hard cheese and creamy goat cheese to make the perfect picnic roll. Australians and New Zealanders love spicy Asian tastes—like chiles and fresh ginger—and they make a perfect match with cheese flavors.

red hot cheese roll-ups

3¼ cups all-purpose flour

1 teaspoon salt, preferably sea salt

1 teaspoon hot red pepper flakes

a few grinds of black pepper

1⅓ cups tepid water

0.6 oz. cake compressed yeast*

1 tablespoon olive oil

cheese filling

3½ oz. creamy, well-flavored goat cheese

⅔ cup coarsely grated mature Cheddar or Monterey Jack cheese

to finish

⅓ cup extra grated Cheddar or Monterey Jack cheese, for sprinkling

a 10-inch round cake pan, greased

makes 9

* To use active dry yeast, mix one ¼ oz. package with the flour, salt, chile flakes, and black pepper; then continue as in the main recipe.

Mix the flour, salt, chile flakes, and black pepper in a large bowl and make a well in the center.

Put half the tepid water into a measuring cup or small bowl, then crumble the yeast over the top. Stir well until dispersed, then pour into the well. Add the rest of the water and the olive oil. Gradually work the flour into the liquid to make a fairly firm dough. If the dough feels sticky, work in extra flour, 1 tablespoon at a time: if there are crumbs at the bottom of the bowl, add a little more water, 1 tablespoon at a time.

Turn out onto a lightly floured work surface and knead thoroughly for 10 minutes until very smooth and elastic. Return the dough to the bowl, cover with plastic wrap, and let rise in a warm place until doubled in size, about 1 hour.

Turn out the risen dough onto a lightly floured work surface and punch down to deflate. Cover the dough with plastic wrap or a dry cloth and let rest for 5 minutes.

Roll out the dough to a rectangle about 16 x 10 inches. Crumble or dot the goat cheese evenly over the dough, then scatter the Cheddar on top.

Starting with the long side, roll up the dough like a jelly roll. Cut the roll into 9 even pieces and arrange them, cut side down and just touching, in the pan. Slip the pan into a plastic bag, then slightly inflate and seal. Let rise as before until almost doubled in size, about 30 minutes.

Meanwhile, preheat the oven to 400°F.

Uncover the rolls, sprinkle with the remaining Cheddar, and bake in the preheated oven for 35 minutes until golden brown. Carefully turn out onto a wire rack to cool.

Eat warm or at room temperature within 24 hours. Can be frozen for up to 1 month. Warm through before serving.

Aborigines who gathered the wild nuts called them "kindall kindall:" the modern name "macadamia" commemorates Dr. John Macadam, who began their commercial cultivation towards the end of the nineteenth century. The trees are native to Australia and are now grown in plantations on the subtropical Queensland coast. Australian lexia raisins are huge, plump, and juicy, almost identical to the American variety, Thompson Seedless raisins from California.

macadamia and lexia raisin bread

Mix the flour, salt, and sugar in a large bowl. Using the tips of your fingers, rub the diced butter into the flour until the mixture looks like fine crumbs. Make a well in the center of the mixture.

Pour the tepid milk and water mixture into a small measuring cup or bowl, crumble the yeast over the top and stir until dispersed. Pour the yeast liquid into the well, then gradually draw in the flour to make a soft, slightly sticky dough. If the dough feels too sticky, work in extra flour, 1 tablespoon at a time: if there are crumbs at the bottom of the bowl, add a little more water, 1 tablespoon at a time.

Turn out onto a lightly floured work surface and knead thoroughly for 10 minutes until firm and very elastic. Gradually work in the raisins and nuts. When thoroughly and evenly distributed through the dough, return it to the bowl. Cover with plastic wrap and let rise in a warm, but not hot, place until doubled in size, about 1 hour.

Turn out the risen dough onto a lightly floured work surface and punch down to deflate. Shape the loaf into a cylinder to fit your pan. Slip the pan into a large plastic bag, inflate slightly, seal, then let rise until doubled in size, about 45 minutes– 1 hour in a warm kitchen.

Meanwhile, preheat the oven to 350°F.

Bake the risen loaf in the preheated oven for about 1 hour until it turns a golden brown and sounds hollow when turned out of the pan and tapped underneath. Cool on a wire rack.

Best eaten the next day, thickly sliced and spread with butter or soft cheese. This bread does not freeze very well.

3 cups all-purpose flour

1 teaspoon salt, preferably sea salt

¼ cup light brown sugar

6 tablespoons unsalted butter, diced

¾ cup tepid milk mixed with ½ cup tepid water

0.6 oz. cake compressed yeast*

1¼ cups raisins

⅔ cup macadamia nuts, lightly toasted and coarsely chopped

a standard loaf pan, 9 x 5 x 3 inches, well greased

makes 1 medium loaf

* To use active dry yeast, mix one ¼ oz. package with the flour, salt, and sugar, then rub in the butter and continue as in the main recipe.

Pumpkin is a favorite ingredient in Australia and New Zealand—as a roasted vegetable, in curries, and in baking. Pumpkin biscuits are a great classic, and pumpkin makes marvelous moist bread too. The cranberries are a contribution from my American family.

pumpkin rolls

1½ lb. eating pumpkin or winter squash

3 tablespoons unsalted butter

2 teaspoons salt, preferably sea salt

3 tablespoons sugar

0.6 oz. cake compressed yeast*

1 tablespoon tepid water

2⅓ cups all-purpose flour

½ teaspoon ground allspice

¼ teaspoon freshly grated nutmeg

1 cup fresh cranberries, or frozen and thawed

½ cup pecan or walnut pieces

1 egg beaten with a pinch of salt, to glaze

a baking sheet, greased

makes 1 medium loaf or 12 rolls

* To use active dry yeast, mix one ¼ oz. package with the flour, then work in the pumpkin mixture. If the dough seems dry or there are crumbs in the bottom of the bowl work in a little tepid water, 1 tablespoon at a time.

Cut the pumpkin in half, then in quarters. Using a very sharp knife, and working on small sections at a time, cut off and discard the skin. Remove and discard the seeds and stringy bits. Chop the flesh into ½-inch chunks—you will need 14 oz. Without adding any water, cook the pumpkin in a steamer or microwave until the pieces soften. Cool slightly, then transfer to a food processor and blend with the butter, salt, and sugar until smooth and creamy. Cool until tepid.

Crumble the yeast into a small bowl, add the water, and stir until smooth and creamy.

Put the flour and spices into a large bowl and make a well in the center. Add the pumpkin purée and yeast mixture to the well, mix briefly, then gradually work in the flour to make a soft but not sticky dough. Depending on your pumpkin and the brand of flour, if the dough is dry, or there are crumbs in the bottom of the bowl, you may need to work in extra tepid water, 1 tablespoon at a time: if the dough sticks to your fingers, add a little extra flour, about 1 tablespoon at a time.

Turn out onto a floured work surface and knead thoroughly for 5 minutes. Return the dough to the bowl, then cover with plastic wrap and let rise at normal room temperature until doubled in size, about 1 hour. Turn out the risen dough onto a lightly floured work surface and work in the cranberries and nuts.

If making a single loaf, shape the dough into a round loaf about 7 inches across and set it on the prepared baking sheet. If making rolls, divide the dough into 12 pieces and pat into roughly shaped balls. Slip the baking sheet into a large plastic bag, slightly inflated, seal, then let rise as before until doubled in size, about 45 minutes if making a single loaf, or 30 minutes if making rolls.

Meanwhile, preheat the oven to 400°F.

If making a single loaf, press your thumb into the center of the risen loaf to make a small hollow, then carefully brush the loaf with the egg glaze. Score the loaf into segments with a sharp knife, to resemble a pumpkin, then bake until the loaf is golden brown and sounds hollow when tapped underneath, about 35 minutes. Cool on a wire rack.

If making rolls, cook them in the preheated oven for about 15–20 minutes or until they sound hollow when tapped underneath. Cool on a wire rack. Best eaten within 3 days.

mail order directory

flour mills

The Baker's Catalogue: King Arthur Flour Company
PO Box 876
Norwich, VT 05055-0876
Tel 1-800-827-6836.
www.kingarthurflour.com
For the dedicated baker—everything you could possibly want. Massive range of flours, grains, seeds, yeasts, equipment. Available by mail order, on-line, or from their store. Produced by the King Arthur flour company. Store is open daily (not holidays). Phone 802-649-3361.

Brunwell Milling
328 East Second Street
Sumner, LA 50674
Tel 319-578-8106
Stone-ground organic bread flours, rye, spelt, and cornmeal. Phone for details and price list.

Butte Creek Mill
P.O. Box 561
Eagle Point, OR 97524
Tel 503-826-3531
Stone-ground bread flour, buckwheat, and cornmeal. Phone for details and price list.

Gray's Grist Mill
P.O. Box 422
Adamsville RI 02801.
Tel/fax 508-636-6075.
Organic and stone-ground flours and cornmeal from mill and by mail order. A favorite with top chefs and bakers. Phone for details and opening times.

The Great Valley Mills
R.D. 3, Country Line Road
Box 1111
Barto, PA 19504
Tel 800-688-6455
Good range of stone-ground bread flour, rye, and semolina flours. Phone for mail order details.

New Hope Mills
RR2, P.O. Box 269A
Moravia NY 13118
Tel 315-497-0783
Stone-ground bread flours, cornmeal, rye, and spelt flours. Phone for details and mail order catalog.

War Eagle Mill
Route 5, Box 411
Rogers AR 72756
Tel 501-789-5343
Stone-ground organic bread flours, rye, buckwheat, and cornmeal. Phone for details and mail order catalog.

bakeware and utensils

The Baker's Catalogue: King Arthur Flour Company
PO Box 876,
Norwich, VT 05055-0876.
Tel 1- 800-827-6836.
www.kingarthurflour.com
Details as left: bakeware and utensils, specialist baker's equipment, and ingredients. Available by mail order, on-line, or from their store.

Dean & Deluca
560 Broadway
New York, NY 10012
and other locations nationwide
Tel 800-221-7714
www.deananddeluca.com
Speciality bakeware and equipment plus ingredients. Mail order available.

Williams-Sonoma
P.O. Box 7456
San Francisco CA 94120-7456
Tel 800-541-2233
www.williams-sonoma.com
Excellent bakeware and tools, some ingredients. Available from mail order catalog or their many stores.

Sur la Table
2 dozen stores nationwide
Tel 1-800 243 0852
www.surlatable.com

Professional Cutlery Direct
Tel 1-800-859-6994
www.cutlery.com

index

picture credits

p. 18 Tony Stone Images, Paul Harris
p. 46 Jacqui Hurst
p. 100 The Anthony Blake Photo
Library, Patrick Syder
p. 116 Lonely Planet Images, Damien
Simonis
p. 128 Ian Wallace

conversion charts

Weights and measures have been rounded up
or down slightly to make measuring easier.

volume equivalents

american	metric	imperial
1 teaspoon	5 ml	
1 tablespoon	15 ml	
¼ cup	60 ml	2 fl.oz.
⅓ cup	75 ml	2½ fl.oz.
½ cup	125 ml	4 fl.oz.
⅔ cup	150 ml	5 fl.oz. (¼ pint)
¾ cup	175 ml	6 fl.oz.
1 cup	250 ml	8 fl.oz.

weight equivalents:

imperial	metric
1 oz.	25 g
2 oz.	50 g
3 oz.	75 g
4 oz.	125 g
5 oz.	150 g
6 oz.	175 g
7 oz.	200 g
8 oz. (½ lb.)	250 g
9 oz. 275 g	
10 oz.	300 g
11 oz.	325 g
12 oz.	375 g
13 oz.	400 g
14 oz.	425 g
15 oz.	475 g
16 oz. (1 lb.)	500 g
2 lb.	1 kg

measurements:

inches	cm
¼ inch	5 mm
½ inch	1 cm
¾ inch	1.5 cm
1 inch	2.5 cm
2 inches	5 cm
3 inches	7 cm
4 inches	10 cm
5 inches	12 cm
6 inches	15 cm
7 inches	18 cm
8 inches	20 cm
9 inches	23 cm
10 inches	25 cm
11 inches	28 cm
12 inches	30 cm

oven temperatures:

225°F	110°C	Gas ¼
250°F	120°C	Gas ½
275°F	140°C	Gas 1
300°F	150°C	Gas 2
325°F	160°C	Gas 3
350°F	180°C	Gas 4
375°F	190°C	Gas 5
400°F	200°C	Gas 6
425°F	220°C	Gas 7
450°F	230°C	Gas 8
475°F	240°C	Gas 9